BASICS
FASHION MANAGEMENT

Virginia Grose

01

FASHION
MERCHANDISING

ethical: aware-
ness/
reflect-
ion/
debate

ava
academia

An AVA Book

Published by AVA Publishing SA
Rue des Fontenailles 16
Case Postale
1000 Lausanne 6
Switzerland
Tel: +41 786 005 109
Email: enquiries@avabooks.com

Distributed by Thames & Hudson (ex-North America)
181a High Holborn
London WC1V 7QX
United Kingdom
Tel: +44 20 7845 5000
Fax: +44 20 7845 5055
Email: sales@thameshudson.co.uk
www.thamesandhudson.com

Distributed in the USA & Canada by:
Ingram Publisher Services Inc.
1 Ingram Blvd.
La Vergne TN 37086
USA
Tel: +1 866 400 5351
Fax: +1 800 838 1149
Email: customer.service@ingrampublisherservices.com

English Language Support Office
AVA Publishing (UK) Ltd.
Tel: +44 1903 204 455
Email: enquiries@avabooks.com

ISBN 978-2-940411-34-4

Library of Congress Cataloging-in-Publication Data
Grose, Virginia.
Basics Fashion Management 01: Fashion Merchandising / Virginia Gross p. cm.
Includes bibliographical references and index.
ISBN: 9782940411344 (pbk.:alk.paper)
eISBN: 9782940447152
1.Fashion merchandising.2.Clothing trade--Study and teaching.3.Fashion design--Study and teaching.
HD9940 .A2 G767 2011

10 9 8 7 6 5 4 3 2 1

Design by Pony Ltd.
www.ponybox.co.uk

Production by AVA Book Production Pte. Ltd., Singapore
Tel: +65 6334 8173
Fax: +65 6259 9830
Email: production@avabooks.com.sg

1 CAREERS IN FASHION
MANAGEMENT

New roles are continually
being created in the fashion
industry, from buyers and
merchandisers to product
developers, sourcing managers,
textile and fabric technologists.
Today's graduates have more
opportunities than ever before.

TABLE OF CONTENTS

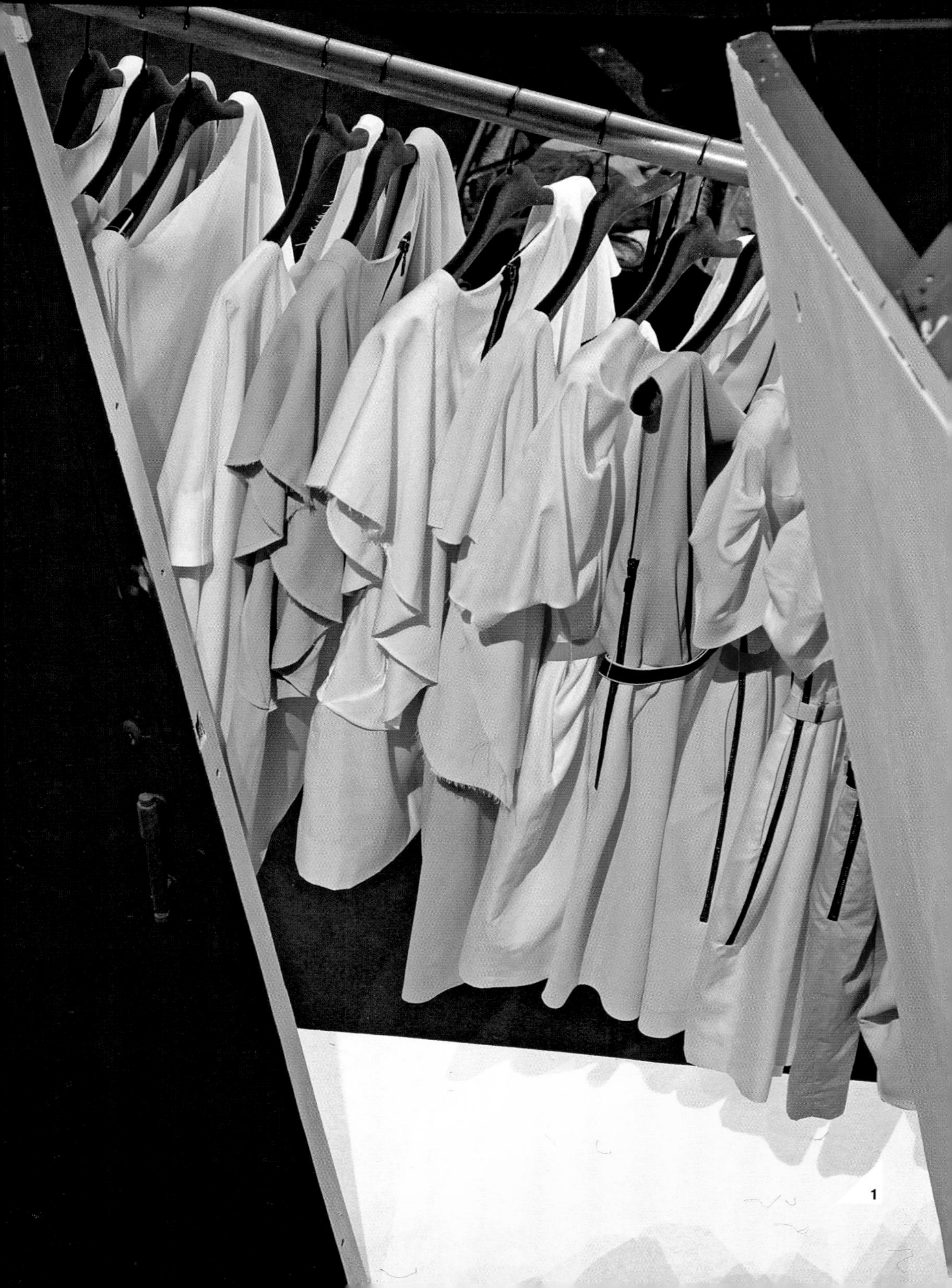

1

INTRODUCTION

The fashion industry encompasses anything sold in a fashion retail store, which may (or may not) have a recognizable brand name. Fashion designers are both product managers and innovators; they might work on a freelance or an independent basis or as part of a larger design team, such as in a retail business or within the supply chain at a manufacturer's or agent's headquarters. But the business of fashion is not built on the design function alone: areas such as forecasting, product development, manufacturing, retailing, marketing, branding and promotion combine to create a multi-billion dollar industry that employs millions worldwide.

Much like the products and designs that are created, each function within this vast industry is unique. Even at the end of a major global recession, new markets continue to open up in the fashion industry because customers still want to grab a bargain, purchase something unique to wear or be seen wearing the latest trends. Fashion design and product development adds value to a retailer or fashion brand's business. However, the industry needs innovation, generated at the same rate as product consumption, or it will become stale; the fashion industry is one that plans for its products to become obsolete at the end of each season.

'Innovation occurs as a result of the interaction of the market, science and an organization's capabilities.'
Trott, 2005

1 FASHION RETAIL

The fashion industry is made up of the design, production and retail of seasonal ranges. By its very nature, fashion becomes obsolete at the end of each season, which feeds the industry and keeps the cycle moving.

Introduction

The fashion business continues to evolve as retailers create new roles within the industry; buyers and merchandisers, product developers, sourcing managers, textile and fabric technologists are some of the industry's key roles. All of this means that for today's graduates there are many opportunities for varied career paths in the fashion business; all over the world and within different types of organization. The speed of this evolution has highlighted a number of emerging, important, considerations for the industry, including issues surrounding sustainability and ethics. The appetite for fast fashion set by certain brands is yet to slow down, as too is consumer enthusiasm for designer goods and branded products within the luxury goods sector. These consumer trends have emerged in the last decade and look set to continue in the foreseeable future.

The business of fashion might be viewed as a critical path and each milestone in it, from concept to customer, is specifically designed to add value to the product. The key stages in this critical path are:

- × Concept, trend and idea generation
- × Design strategy
- × Design and product development
- × Retail strategy
- × Fabric development
- × Sampling
- × Range planning
- × Sourcing strategy
- × Production
- × Shipping
- × Distribution
- × Promotion
- × Sales
- × Customer reaction

THE FASHION BUSINESS: A CRITICAL PATH

RESEARCH
AND IDEA
GENERATION   RANGE PLANNING   FABRIC AND YARN
                                                               DEVELOPMENT

            INITIAL CONCEPT   RANGE DESIGNS   SAMPLE SIGN-OFF
                                               SIGN-OFF

This is a generic pathway: every fashion retailer or brand will adapt and develop its own version of these stages to ensure that they are tailored to the requirements of its product ranges and customer base.

The aim of this book is to recreate this blueprint for fashion design, marketing, buying and merchandising so that you gain an appreciation of the critical path and key stages of the fashion business. Each of the five chapters explores a milestone in the fashion pathway. To help bring the theory to life and make the content immediately accessible, each chapter also contains a relevant case study and an interview with an industry professional. There are also self-reflective questions and exercises at the end of each chapter to help you to develop their ideas further.

MANUFACTURING

DISTRIBUTION
TO STORES

SALES AND
CUSTOMER
EXPERIENCE

SHIPMENT
OF BULK
PRODUCTION

VISUAL
MERCHANDISING

1

CONTEXT AND CONCEPT

1

This chapter will provide an insight into the creative activities and design concepts of the fashion process. The creative activities in any business setting will form part of a broader operational process that is designed to turn innovative and intangible ideas into a profitable reality. The fashion industry is no exception. Creating fashion is an exciting, challenging and, at times, risky business, but this highly creative industry is underpinned by a solid business model and operational workflow. It is important to bear in mind that any retailer is in the fashion business to make a profit, and that fashion is a for-profit industry like any other.

1 PETER PILOTTO AW10

Fashion designers and the concepts they create form the starting point of the industry's pathway. The designer is the crucial link in the chain of buyers, merchandisers and apparel manufacturers.

From couture to high street

The process of the fashion business remains much the same now as when Charles Frederick Worth introduced the concept of haute couture in the 1850s: an idea is sketched to start the ball rolling, samples are made, then the garments are manufactured and sold to individual or mass-market customers.

Haute couture and prêt-à-porter

Haute couture specifically refers to the design and construction of high-quality clothes by leading fashion houses. In its purest form, the term is a protected appellation. A certain number of formal criteria (such as number of employees or participation in fashion shows) must be met for a fashion house to use the label. Christian Dior, Chanel and Givenchy are all haute couture design houses. In broader usage, the term couture is used to describe all custom-made clothing.

Couture designers and design houses occupy a highly influential position in the fashion process; they are often the first to identify and capture a trend, concept or theme, which other designers and stakeholders in the fashion business then emulate for creative or commercial gain. Many of the pieces that couture designers create are arguably works of art. These creations are eventually translated into wearable, commercial and fashionable clothes that are suitable for mass market consumption. To keep the fashion business cycle in motion, it is essential to invest in and nurture the talent and innovation of pure creative designers at this level.

Charles Frederick Worth (1826–1895)

Credited with introducing the concept of haute couture, Charles Worth was known for preparing designs that were shown on live models and tailor-made for clients in his workshop. Worth was not the first or only designer to organize his business in this way, but his aggressive self-promotion earned him recognition as the first 'couturier'.

'Often what seems to be intuition is actually clever assimilation and analysis of careful research.'
Gini Stephens Frings, 2002

1

Christian Dior
no 55
manteau lainage
noir
et col castor

2

Prêt-à-porter (ready-to-wear) clothing lines were the first radical alternative to couture pieces when they hit boutiques in the 1960s. The term describes factory-made clothing that is sold in finished condition and in standardized sizes (as distinct from bespoke, made-to-measure haute couture). Yves Saint Laurent (YSL) is credited as being the first French haute couturier to come out with a full prêt-à-porter line; some attribute this decision as a wish to democratize fashion, although other couture houses were preparing prêt-à-porter lines at the same time. The first Rive Gauche stores, which sold the YSL prêt-à-porter line, opened in Paris in 1966.

Ready-to-wear has rather different connotations in the spheres of fashion and classic clothing. In the fashion industry, designers produce ready-to-wear clothes that are intended to be worn without significant alteration, because clothing made to standard sizes will fit most people. Standard patterns and faster construction techniques are used to keep costs down, compared to a custom-sewn version of the same item. Some fashion houses and designers offer mass-produced, industrially manufactured ready-to-wear lines, while others offer garments that, while not unique, are produced in limited numbers.

The influence of couture houses and designers has changed over time. Nowadays, only a very small clientele can afford the time and expense demanded by true couture clothing. Instead, the iconic fashion houses of Chanel, Givenchy, Dior, Versace, Ralph Lauren and Armani make a larger proportion of their profits from licensing agreements on cosmetics, perfume and accessories. For example, Chanel's Rouge Noir lipstick and nail polish brought the House of Chanel to the masses and sales of its cosmetics and perfume are worth billions of dollars.

1+2 NEW LOOK

Christian Dior's New Look (1947) was controversial because the collection used vast amounts of fabric in a period when wartime rationing was still in effect. Christian Dior defined a new business model in the post-war years, establishing ready-to-wear boutiques and licensing deals; his designs were copied and sold in the USA as well as Europe. Many consider Dior's model to be a forerunner of fast fashion.

From couture to high street

Fast fashion: the high-street revolution

Although we tend to think of fast fashion as a new industry initiative, it is in fact a redevelopment and refinement of Yves Saint Laurent's prêt-à-porter business model. Chain store retailers began to emerge in the 1960s, such as Mary Quant, Chelsea Girl and Biba in the UK and Levi Strauss and Gap in the USA.

Today's top designers, many of whom are now household names, can influence the fashion industry as a whole. Designer brands such as Giorgio Armani, Calvin Klein and Ralph Lauren are examples of such large businesses that develop products for the mass market via their diffusion ranges and high-street collaborations. The distinction between high-end and mass market fashion is blurring as collaborations between designers and high-street stores become increasingly commonplace. This trend looks set to continue, driven as it is by high consumer demand for fast fashion. These days, if the masses cannot afford the original then the designers are prepared to go the masses.

The fashion industry is one of the few industries to provide advance photographs (usually via the Internet) of its new product ranges and, by doing so, it can be argued that couture houses are providing some form of service to the high-street fashion retailers via their creative influence. The media and fashion press are responsible for editing the collections and presenting trends along with the catwalk spreads and advance product information in their publications. Such catwalk creations are then filtered down (at increasing speed) to fashion retail. Many fashion and mainstream magazines, for example, will regularly feature 'copycat' sections, showing the public where to find cheaper, replica versions of designer items.

1+2 DESIGNER CREATIONS AND HIGH-STREET COPYCATS

Something that begins its life on a drawing board at a fashion house may easily become a derivative version in Target, H&M or Topshop, and Stella McCartney's lemon-print dress (2011) is a good example of this. This distinctive design was interpreted by high-street design teams (such as this one, by Primark), making it suitable for mass production at an affordable purchase price.

2

'The fashion cycle is a little bit of an anachronism. We still show clothes in February and they're not available until July or August or September. By that point, images of the collection have been seen all over the Internet and discussed ad nauseum on blogs and social networks and on Style.com, and by the time it reaches the store, people are already [tired of it], it's done. The fashion cycle does not fit with the speed of communication. Instead of showing things on the runway [that won't be in stores for several months] we should be showing things that can be bought right away. Net-a-porter did this well with Roland Mouret and Halston. Instead of being more responsive, we're doing more seasons and more collections, and that's not the solution, the solution is to give people what they want when they want it.'
Women's Wear Daily, 2009

Designer typology

Fashion designers develop new concepts and, as part of the creative process, are responsible for delivering these concepts in the form of fashionable clothing designs. There are different types of fashion designers and fashion retailers worldwide and they work in different segments of the market, such as fashion branding, design houses or high-street retail. Designers from different sectors of the fashion business will influence one another; they are inextricably linked by the design process and take inspiration from everything that they come into contact with.

Rieple and Gander (2009) conducted research on the typology of fashion designers and arrived at the conclusion that there are four classifications into which most apparel designers fall: mavericks, leaders, interpreters and reproducers.

Mavericks

Mavericks are purely creative (rather than commercial) designers and often assume the role of creative design director or trend-forecasting consultant. Mavericks advise top design houses on seasonal directions for colour, style and fabric choices. These designers are not primarily concerned with current consumer or market trends; they will instead create couture, new looks and direction for a brand, preferring to lead rather than follow. Examples of contemporary mavericks include John Galliano, Vivienne Westwood and Alexander McQueen (it will be interesting to see how the company attempts to replace his design flair following his death in 2010).

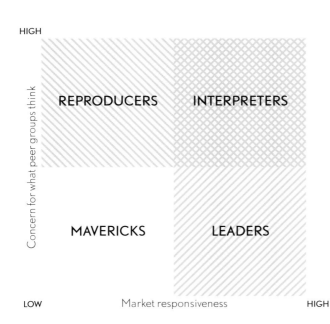

1   A TYPOLOGY OF APPAREL DESIGNERS

Designers are inextricably linked by the design process and each other. Research by Rieple and Gander focuses on designer typology and how co-locating with other designers and creative organizations allows them to draw upon a number of intangible resources such as street scenes, social moods and atmosphere in order to create new designs.
[Source: Rieple & Gander 2009]

HIGH

Concern for what peer groups think

REPRODUCERS   INTERPRETERS

MAVERICKS   LEADERS

LOW   Market responsiveness   HIGH

Leaders

Fashion leaders are 'top-end' designers who become recognizable names during the course of their career by either working for other fashion houses (such as Donna Karan for Anne Klein) or by setting up a commercial, rather than purely creative, business model. Leaders innovate in a highly fashionable and groundbreaking manner and will often establish their own label; for example, designer Tom Ford went on to develop his own label following his time at Gucci.

Interpreters

Interpreters have assumed a relatively new role in fashion. They are neither designers nor buyers or product developers, but a hybrid of all three. These individuals have a commercial eye and are primarily concerned with selecting the key looks for a season. Interpreters work closely with the merchandising and technical aspects of the business and will focus their energies on the way in which a brand or retailer communicates their design message to consumers.

Examples of companies that employ interpreters include Karen Millen, Anthropologie and Banana Republic. Additionally, large multiples or retailer brands with in-house labels, such as House of Fraser, JC Penney and The Limited, also employ fashion interpreters.

Reproducers

Reproducers (also known as fast fashion designers) work in conjunction with a team of buyers and product developers, managing the development of the looks for a particular retailer or brand. They ensure that colour palettes and trends of the looks fit with the business or brand. These commercially astute designers need to ensure that whilst the direction is 'fashion right' it is simultaneously wearable and cost-effective.

Reproducers source, select and adapt ideas and trends to suit a particular segment of the market. It is arguably not a highly creative role, yet it is a technically skilful one required to highlight those catwalk trends that will successfully translate to the high street. High-street retailers such as H&M, Zara, Gap and Forever 21 employ reproducers.

'The best way to predict the future is to create it.'
Peter Drucker

Research and idea generation

The creative process of fashion design does not have a fixed start or end point; it is an iterative one and fashion designers often display magpie tendencies by constantly seeking and collecting sources of inspiration in order to rework, evolve and advance their ideas in a cyclical way. Sources of inspiration may include a scrap of fabric, a flash of colour, a trip to another city or country, or an exhibition; equally, there may be an accumulation of different ideas gathered over time.

Sources of inspiration and their personal interpretation, both visually and technically, play an important part in increasing creativity in the design process (Fatme, 2006). Inspiration and where it comes from is the very essence of the fashion design process and continual research is a critically important success factor in developing and determining new design concepts.

Commercial fashion designers have to conceive and develop clothing ranges and remain creative whilst working closely with buyers, merchandisers and senior managers in order to successfully channel a company's message and philosophy into its clothing. The process involves analysing key trends from the catwalk shows and identifying opportunities to translate these ideas into clothing that will fit a company's brand.

Forecasting trends and developing inspired ideas based upon information gathered is not new. It is vital to fashion designers to find continual new sources of inspiration. Originality and flair are key prerequisites for a fashion designer's creativity. These intangible qualities cannot be easily taught and are instead forged by a designer's intuition and translated into their clothing style, which makes research and trend forecasting such an exciting area of the creative process.

1

2

Market analysis and research

The behaviour of customers dictates to retailers how to develop successful new products and gives a great insight (if correctly analysed) into customer shopping habits and behaviour. Historical data has often been a dictator of future trends so it should be no surprise that the creative process in fashion retailing often begins with analysing consumer trend data, sales information and customer feedback from the previous season. Retailers also routinely consult market research reports (such as those written by <www.mintel.com> or <www.verdict.co.uk>) in order to define the competition and further analyse the market and environmental trend factors that are most relevant to their customers. Market research provides an invaluable insight into the industry; the data is combined with other key macro-environmental influences (the key drivers affecting both the retailer or business and its customers) to help designers capture the spirit of the times, the fashion **zeitgeist,** when developing their collections (Stone, 2001).

1+2 FABRIC AND COLOUR FAIRS: PITTI IMMAGINE FILATI

Pitti Immagine Filati showcases yarns and colour trends to an audience of international buyers and designers who come to the Florence trade fair looking for new creative ideas.

The fashion zeitgeist can further be defined by:

× A designer's signature or style influence (such as Tom Ford at Gucci)

× A style icon or celebrity (such as Madonna or Victoria Beckham)

× A fashion look, maybe created by film or TV (think of Carrie from *Sex and the City*)

× A bohemian element found in music or street culture (such as punk)

× A fashion model (for example, Kate Moss or Elle Macpherson)

× Advances in fibre or fabric technology (for example, Lycra developments in the 1970s made body-conscious clothing fashionable)

(Source: E L Brannon, 2005)

Research and idea generation

Colour information

In addition to customer and market research, design teams will visit yarn and fabric **trade fairs** and attend colour seminars ahead of each season in order to compile initial colour palettes and fabric and trim ideas for their range planning. It is vital to have this research information to hand when fashion designers are putting pen to paper so that as silhouettes are developed, they are linked to and supported by the appropriate fabric and trim information. The initial design, concept and product development processes do not work independently of one another.

TRADE FAIRS

The following key fashion, fabric, yarn and product fairs help determine the look of any given season. Most are bi-annual, falling in January/February and September/October.

× London Fashion Week
× Paris Fashion Week
× New York Fashion Week
× Milan Fashion Week
× Tokyo Fashion Week
× Première Vision (Paris, France)
× Pitti Filati (Florence, Italy)
× Interfilière (Paris and Lyon, France)
× Magic (Las Vegas, USA)
× Expofil (Paris, France)
× Moda-Pelle (Milan, Italy)

1+2 FABRIC AND COLOUR FAIRS: PITTI IMMAGINE FILATI

Trade fairs are an essential part of research process. Designers will attend yarn and fabric trade fairs in order to compile colour and fabric palettes for the forthcoming season. Pitti Immagine's mission statement is to continuously review the approach to trade fairs and cultural programmes, to promote fashion and art on an international level, interpreting different cultures and bringing them together.

1

Directional and comparative shopping

Shopping takes on a whole new meaning for commercial designers. At the beginning of any fashion season, designers travel (often extensively) to trade fairs, designer, high street and vintage stores and street markets in order to seek out ideas from around the globe. This is directional shopping. Notes and photographs will be taken and samples bought for further analysis of fabric trim or styling direction. Often garments will be deconstructed (literally ripped apart) to analyse and test fabrics so that they may be redeveloped and recreated into mass market products.

Comparative shopping and competitive analysis helps buyers and commercial designers to determine the retailer's position in the marketplace; the process highlights similarities or differences between a retailer and its competition. Factors such as price, styling and quality will be observed and reviewed, as will any promotional activity. Comparative shopping provides a snapshot of the high street – the competition – and it is an important part of the commercial design process.

2

Research and idea generation

FASHION AT WORK

1

Trends in the marketplace

In any commercial environment, trends in the marketplace will help shape the future direction of the business and help the organization to fulfil the needs and desires of the customer. The fashion business is no exception. Trends in business can be broadly categorized in one of three ways: macro, micro and megatrends.

Macro or environmental trends are driven by long-term societal, global and political forces, often referred to as the PESTEL model, representing political, economic, sociological, technological, environmental and legal forces. The retailer or company will decide which of these factors are the likely drivers or forces that will influence the whole of society and therefore individual customer behaviour. These trends can evolve over a long period of time, gather momentum and may be hugely influential for retailers. See more on the PESTEL model in chapter 3, page 70.

Micro trends are more immediate; they can create a lot of interest or noise but tend to disappear as quickly as they arrive. The fashion industry is particularly affected and shaped by micro trends. These can be weather-related, such as snow or a heatwave, or may be blips or fads that take off and die quickly. A good example of a fashion-related micro trend that suddenly evolved was the 'jeggings' trend, a cross between skinny jeans and leggings.

Macro and micro trends can evolve into what are widely known as megatrends. A megatrend will last longer, affect greater aspects of society than either macro or micro trends and they may involve a complex process that can include global economic forces, political persuasions and technological advances. Megatrends have a lasting influence on society and can be unpredictable (Vejlgaard, 2007). Indeed, according to Vejlgaard, there are certain sectors of society that have historically driven (and continue to drive) megatrend development, such as the young, sub-cultures, artists, the wealthy or super-rich, designers, celebrities and the media. A good example of a megatrend is ethical fashion, which has been evolving for over ten years.

Customer behaviour and segmentation

Commercial fashion design and retailing starts and ends with the customer. The customer is at the centre of all design developments and, simply put, the fashion business is the creation, interpretation and development of ideas to suit customers' needs. It is vital to keep this in mind: customer behaviour and consumer spending patterns drive the fashion industry.

Customer needs can be unpredictable, but it is important for designers to analyse sales and spending patterns as well as understand the key drivers of customer behaviour as part of the range development process. For example, one of the biggest influences in the last decade on customer behaviour has been the Internet and designers and retailers alike have had to adapt in order to integrate technological advances in their ranges and in their business models. Developing bespoke products in fashion design and producing clothing that is suitable for customers, at the right price, is a continual challenge for fashion brands and retailers.

2

1+2 FASHION AT WORK

It is important to remember that the fashion industry is a commercial, for-profit business like any other and it begins and ends with the customer. Research into consumer behaviour and spending patterns drives the creation and development of innovative fashion to suit customer needs.

Trend forecasting

1

The initial stages of the idea generation and range planning process are shaped by the fashion industry in the form of trend forecasting companies, major trade fairs and international trade panels that predict colour, fabric and styling for the season ahead. Trend forecasting is a vital part of the fashion design process; it provides the fuel in the fashion engine.

Professional trend forecasters provide an invaluable service to fashion retailers and brands, many of whom simply do not have sufficient time or resources to undertake this work in-house. Forecasters employ creative marketing and design consultants to predict trends and gather information for the fashion industry. These consultants will travel the globe seeking out concepts and trends that are taken from a wide range of sources such as music, street style, art, exhibitions, architecture and interior design.

Trend forecasting has become an important function within the fashion industry and it has evolved and changed with fashion itself. Some of the prestigious trend forecasting companies include (but are not limited to): Promostyl, Trend Union and Peclers. These and other trend agencies will forecast everything from colour and styling to fabric and yarn. It is important to note that trend agencies do not forecast the construction of sample garments, which is exclusive to individual businesses and retailers. Retailers of designed products control this segment of the development process by working directly with manufacturers and suppliers.

Trends in colour direction act as a catalyst for further research into fabric and styling. This is noteworthy because it is conducted by a range of international panels and committees, which form a coalition of opinion to enable retailers and manufacturers to make key colour decisions. The International Colour Authority (ICA), founded in 1966, is the world's leading colour forecasting service. The ICA's design consultants meet twice a year to agree on the new colour trends for interiors, exteriors, fashion and all manufactured coloured products.

Trend, colour and fashion forecasters often work two years in advance of the season. Many of these individuals have fashion design backgrounds, but business acumen is equally important, as is an inherent curiosity to seek out the new, the original and the different.

1 PECLERS TRENDBOOKS

French trend agency Peclers was founded by Dominique Peclers in 1970, inspired by her passion for fashion and architecture. It describes itself as a 'buzzing idea lab, generating a constant flow of new ideas and leads'.

'Designers must learn most of all to keep their eyes open, to develop their skills of observation, to absorb visual ideas, blend them and translate into clothes that their customers will want to buy. Exposure to beautiful things helps a designer distinguish genuine beauty and quality from fads and mediocrity.'
Gini Stephens Frings, 2002

Trend forecasting

Cool hunting

Most large organizations and retailers go to great lengths to stay ahead of the competition. One way in which they can do this is to employ 'cool hunters' to seek out trends and innovative ideas; this helps to ensure that they are the first to market with a great new product and can also help the organization develop a long-term strategy for its business.

Driven by a stiff level of market competition and most organizations' desire to get their product quickly to market and 'right' on the first attempt, the role of the cool hunter is rapidly assuming a key position in the fashion business. There are now many web-based forecasting and cool hunting companies or agencies. Brands such as Levi Strauss, Coca Cola and Nike are well known for using cool hunters to work on innovative projects, and retailers including JC Penney are now using their own cool hunters to try to win the innovation race.

Cool hunters will observe and talk to trendsetters from all walks of life in order to find out what sociologists have referred to as the 'tipping point' (Gladwell, 2008) in the process of change. Finding trend spotting clues is very important to fashion designers and retailers. The industry relies upon new product development (or reinvention) and customers in fashion thrive upon 'newness'. The entire industry is driven by the need to stand out from the crowd or look different and original. Websites that promote cool and new trends (from the sublime to the ridiculous) are great places to start looking for inspiration (see <www.coolhunter.com> and <www.trendhunter.com>).

'The industry has used trend forecasts for 40 years, but the forecaster's role has changed substantially from the late 60s and early 70s. Then, forecasters were simply trend-spotters, taking photos and reporting on what people were wearing... today, fashion forecasting is focused as much on market analysis as on spotting street trends.'
David Wolfe

1

1+2 PECLERS TRENDBOOKS

Peclers produces consumer trend forecasts for its clients, who include Prada, Armani, Carrefour, Lancôme, Monoprix, L'Oréal and Nissan, amongst others. The agency is known for its trend books, which are published every season and distributed internationally.

2

Interview: Kim Mannino

KIM MANNINO

1974–1977

studied at the London College of Fashion and gained a diploma in women's dress and light clothing

1977–1979

worked as a sample machinist to supply clothing lines to high-street chain stores

1979–1983

began teaching and lecturing in clothing production

1983–1990

worked in various roles (including garment technologist, sample room manager and production manager) for Katharine Hamnett, The Bureau Design Group, Richard James and Margaret Howell

1990–present

UK Director at Promostyl (international trend research and design agency)

'Fashion retailers should not follow every trend, but really understand the customer and interpret what is right for their target consumers' age group, salary range and likes and dislikes. This is how to keep fashion relevant and individual to the customer.'

Q In your opinion, how has the role of the couture designer changed in the last 20 years to occupy its current, highly influential position in the fashion industry?

A I think it's very interesting. Today, celebrities wear couture designs that filter down to the high street via the press (in magazines such as *Heat* or *Hello*) for the youth market and discounters to pick up on it. Previously, a catwalk collection would take 12–18 months to filter down to the high street. Now it can take as little as six weeks before current catwalk-inspired designs are hanging on the rails on the high street.

The 15–25-year-old age group shopping in the mass market will immediately know what fashion designs they want. This group will see celebrities on TV or in magazines wearing Marc Jacobs or Gucci couture and will want their own fast and inexpensive version of the same designs. Twenty years ago the same age group's consumer demands would not have been generated or realized in the same way. At that time only a certain type of affluent, older and (predominantly) female consumer (who had most probably been informed by *Vogue* magazine) would have a couture-inspired demand for fashion. Now retailers have begun to use the celebrity trend to their advantage and interpret those key looks from the magazines as part of the trend process.

Q Do you think top design houses still influence fashion?

A Yes, but it [their influence] is largely celebrity driven. The fragrance and cosmetics side of their businesses helps keep them in the spotlight.

Interview: Kim Mannino

Q How do you think that designers gather ideas and influences?

A It has changed. A lot of style and trend information is now supplied by Internet-based services. Designers and their design teams now travel far less to the key trend fairs around the world than they used to. Budgets have been cut as many companies subscribe to information services to replace the trendseeking part of the process.

Designers used to only focus on one season at a time and complete one phase prior to developing the next, but now it is four or even six. In addition to this, every retailer or brand seems to spend a great deal of time looking at what the others are doing; at a time when international travel is limited and a lot of trend information is reviewed via the Internet, this will fuel replication in the industry if we are not careful.

There used to be more of a truly seasonal forecast from the leading trend agencies and services, and retailers and brands previously bought into trend direction information and edited it themselves. This service has evolved into constant reportage that is readily available. However, volume and mass markets that have a tendency to focus on the same ideas has created more homogenization and a less individual and unique look of the traditional high street.

Q How you think that yarn and fabric suppliers continue to be a large influence in the concept stages?

A Fabric and yarn suppliers at trade fairs such as Première Vision absolutely influence the design concept stage. In fact, long-term developments in the industry tend to evolve in this way.

'Retailers have begun to use the celebrity trend to their advantage and interpret those key looks from the magazines as part of the trend process.'

Q How does the media influence fashion?

A The media's influence on fashion is bigger than ever. If you wanted to look at fashion in the media 10–15 years ago you would see fewer publications that were far more polarized. At the top end of the range were *Vogue* and *Harper's Bazaar*. Now there are so many to choose from and celebrity culture has created this almost instant access to fashion trends.

Vogue, *Harper's* and similar publications remain serious fashion magazines. But an increasing number of celebrity gossip magazines that contain pictures of stars wearing whatever makes a huge amount of fashion information available to the public at large. As such, mass-market fashion is increasingly driven by the media and the Internet. The industry will still visit trend shows and fairs, but they will decide upon key looks for their ranges based on what celebrities, as shot by the media, are wearing. Trend forecasting books and publications are increasingly a confirmation of trend directions.

Q Given that colour forecasts tend to be conducted well in advance of a given season, do they remain relevant in the business of trend directions?

A They are definitely relevant and essential and it is important that we pay attention to how colour forecasts are used and interpreted. How colour information is used and harmonized has changed in the last 15–20 years. At that time, clear colour directions would be set and they would change completely each season. Now, many new hues and tones of the same colour exist, which can change and reinvent themselves from season to season.

Colour direction is constantly in demand and one of the most popular trend direction books bought by international clients (closely followed by shape and womenswear directions). It is important and exciting to predict colour information and direction, and in fact it is a form of forecasting that really does not lend itself easily to the Internet; properly visualizing colour means viewing via Pantone, yarn or fabric swatches to see the true tones.

Every retailer and designer now works very close to the season, but they are often faced with long development times in their manufacturing cycles (increasingly these are located in the Far East). So advanced trend information, and colour predictions in particular, are extremely helpful.

Interview: Kim Mannino

Q Do large, international high-street retailers take their inspiration from catwalks and trade fairs or from prediction companies?

A All of these are forms of inspiration. All of the big international fashion retailers are driven by celebrity culture, media and catwalk collections, as well as trend prediction companies. Trend forecasters used to wait five or six weeks after collections had debuted to receive catwalk looks on slides and clients were then invited to attend presentations at trend agency offices – it all took so long! Now, almost immediately after a catwalk show takes place, designers and retailers are able to view collections online and revisit the looks every day.

However fashion retailers are aware that they need their own points of difference and will conduct their own research. In fact, Première Vision (in September 2009) was so busy that it generated a real feeling of optimism that designers and creative individuals were desperate to gather information in order to get their product right and be individual.

A few companies may say that they do not look at trends, but in truth no one can afford to miss the boat, and it is especially important during times of economic recession; prudent retailers will look at trend research as well as catwalks for inspiration. Consumers make buying decisions carefully when money is tight and it is vitally important that retailers must identify their customer and the market position they hold. Fashion retailers should not follow every trend, but really understand the customer and interpret what is right for their target consumers' age group, salary range and likes and dislikes. This is how to keep fashion relevant and individual to the customer.

Q How do you see trend forecasting in the future?

A It is not an exact science! Trend forecasting companies and agencies are only as successful as the creative teams that run them. They do not often get it wrong, but it has become more difficult to forecast micro trends (such as the 'jegging' hybrid, which evolved from skinny jeans and leggings). In the future there will be more information available at much shorter intervals. The sending out of fast mail shots and e-mailing updates to clients is likely to continue and increase.

Q In the future, how do you see couture fashion and trend forecasting influencing the high street?

A The fashion industry is currently fuelled by the couture houses clothing celebrities under the eye of an ever-watchful media. This may continue to fuel fast fashion, but there are some significant long-term trends developing such as vintage and eco-friendly fashion (these actually sit side by side).

It is important to note that trends swing like a pendulum. For example, the minimalism trend has replaced luxe trends (consumers want to believe they can obtain luxury on the high street) and the sport and street/urban trend, which began around ten years ago, has since become mainstream and disappeared. Trend forecasting is about looking at the bigger design picture (such as cars, architecture, interiors, graphics and illustrations, the history of advertising); ideas and concepts evolve from the environment in general and this is set to continue in the future.

Q How have the initial concepts, which drive designers, changed?

A The designer's initial concept development process remains the same at the top end of the market, but on the high street designers do not have as much time available to them these days to visit museums and exhibitions to seek inspiration. Generally, designers are intuitive and observational individuals who will pick up on the environment around them. You cannot train people to behave like this. Designers have tacit knowledge and often just know what is right for the moment.

'Designers are intuitive and observational individuals who will pick up on the environment around them. You cannot train people to behave like this. Designers have tacit knowledge and often just know what is right for the moment.'

Case study: WGSN

WGSN (Worth Global Style Net) is a London-based Internet trend forecasting agency that has been operating for more than 15 years. The organization aims to provide up-to-date and relevant trend forecasting services via a web-based system. Established by brothers Julian and Marc Worth as a revolutionary forecasting service, primarily for the fashion industry, WGSN now has offices around the world, including New York, Melbourne, Istanbul, Hong Kong and, most recently, Shanghai.

Trend forecasting is an accepted method of information gathering within the fashion and other creative industries. WGSN clients (generally large businesses) pay a fee for certain log-in privileges, which allow them access to catwalk trend information, trend shows, directional changes in street and vintage fashion as well as colour and fabric directions. WGSN provides the fashion business with detailed analysis of business and economic issues in the industry. Its service is of particular interest to mass market design teams and retailers to whom speed is of the essence and time is short. Fashion designers who fit the reproducer and interpreter typology (see page 16) are likely to find WGSN's data invaluable as it is delivered to their desktop and saves them both time and effort in continually gathering up-to-the minute information. WGSN is perhaps less relevant for mavericks and fashion leaders, who will formulate their own trends and are in fact groups that will, by virtue of their level of creativity, drive trends themselves down to the next level.

Until recently, most of the leading fashion forecasting companies were based in Europe, which is thought to be (and some may argue, still is) the birthplace and epicentre of couture and the fashion industry. These more traditional trend forecasting agencies produce beautifully bound books that display styling visuals and fabric, colour and yarn swatches as samples of directional trends for retailers who subscribe to the agency's services.

'[WGSN is] the Bloomberg of fashion.'
Business Week

John Galliano
autumn/winter 2007/08

Miss Haversham from *Great Expectations*, 1946

Tush M

Mourning light
emento mori and curios worn as macabre pendants, bi
flect a very modern obsession with death and the unusua

Mourning Brooch
by Julia deVille

John Galliano
autumn/winter 2007/08

Jean
autumn

Topshop
London

Eric Prydz's *Call on Me* vide

eo, and the accessibility of
braces a **fun, individual**

footwear, soft uppers and
, rounded toe with **shallo**

WGSN TREND FORECASTS

WGSN publishes thousands of news and business stories each year, reporting events and issues in the fashion and style industries as well as predictions tailored for industry professionals.

nsolls remain important: p
l iridescent fabrics, or emb
in their popularity with th
shing prints and bold co

WGSN street shot, Londor

sculine lace-up styles beco
ks emerging as a major

t white or black leather ja
ed with boldly-patterned h
htly more structured shap

henticity is important for I
ssic dancewear retailers (s
n scuffed and laceless, or
warmers and scrunched sp
tors, tap-shoe eyelet- and

Tony Maggs, Rockabaret Club

London   New York

New York

London's **Rockabaret Club** is s...
in the theatrical environs of a...

Bergdorf Goodman   Topshop
New York   New Yor...

...ed and

Saturday of the month in the
Grand Ballroom of the Cobden
Club.

www.rockabaret.co.uk

...n Apparel casualwear, Aerobicise

...WGSN street shot, Hong Kong

...are key. Shapes mix the ubiquitous
...gynous styles and low or flat heels.

...styles are overhauled with metallic
...loured sequins. Ballet shoes also
...for spring/summer, moved on by

Freed of London

...with **jazz-pump and dance-shoe**
...l sectors.

...voke modern-dance nostalgia when
...s and socks, or formalised with a
...oden heel.

...et, with **traditional tap shoes** from
...London) **adapted as streetwear:**
...es, and paired with tights,
...ixed with jeans. Across other
...nhance the appeal of formal styles.

Kate Bush

Jane Fonda

- Aerobicise icons inclu...
  Bush and Jane Fonda...

Fame soundtrac...

WGSN for the high street

So how might a high-street fashion designer typically use
WGSN's services? Primarily, it forms part of the analysis
and research phase while designers develop their concept
and initial ideas for a typical season. Designers who
reproduce and interpret information continually will log in
to the services and receive the daily updates that are most
appropriate for the brand and the customers they represent.

WGSN's staff attend the major trade fairs and report back
on colour and fabric and product directions. In particular,
the seasonal runway shows are well reported and made
immediately available via WGSN's websites to brand and
retailer clients.

WGSN also offers its own interpretation of the key global
and localized trends from the music industry, vintage stores,
interior design and many other fields, from which designers
develop range ideas, incorporating them within their own
concept mood boards. WGSN edits its findings before
posting them online, making it easy for clients to interpret.
The information is divided by product type or market
section making the content quick and easy to navigate.
WGSN's trend categorization includes:

- ×   Women
- ×   Men
- ×   Children
- ×   Accessories
- ×   Vintage
- ×   Colour
- ×   Trade fair updates
- ×   Global shop reports
- ×   Business news
- ×   Think tank (a section of topical discussion points)

Case study: WGSN

WGSN: part of the fast fashion research process

Mass-market fashion retailers such as H&M, Zara, Primark and Topshop have perfected the art of fast fashion. As its name suggests, fast fashion is a fast moving industry with manufacturing and supply chains that have to operate both quickly and efficiently despite some distance between component parts of the chain. These companies rely heavily on agency trend information and their in-house fashion designers depend upon the services of WGSN to quickly visualize and interpret key looks and styling from catwalks and couture design houses. These designers will review and utilize the trend information in order to compile initial ideas for their mood boards and to quickly assemble colour and trend directions for that season (all without actually having to visit the shows). This is the first stage of the designer's range planning process and these visual aids also serve as communication tools in key discussions that the designers will have with buyers and merchandisers. The results of these discussions will help a retailer determine the most appropriate direction to take in order to further develop its product range in line with customer demands and expectations; this forms the basis of the retailer's design strategy and will be referred to and adapted by the team from this point forward.

WGSN's service is not just prescriptive: it can aid inspiration and add weight to conceptual ideas and directional trends that designers may already have, but need help formalizing into something more tangible. It is important to note that gathering and monitoring information from a company such as WGSN is part of an ongoing process for fast fashion retailers and this high-speed access to trend forecasting data is vital.

WGSN TREND FORECASTS

WGSN supplies trend forecasts and analysis to 36,000 customers across the apparel, style, design and retail industries. Its 200-strong team of creative and editorial staff are based in London, with offices worldwide.

'[WGSN's] skill lies in good editing of information of styling, trends and by remaining relevant to its global users. It is currently developing an electronic mood board for users as well as translating its site into Mandarin and it seems unstoppable. WGSN has been accused of homogenizing fashion to the detriment of creativity, but the service merely ensures that designers keep up with the dizzying pace of trends.'
M Carter, 2009

The user is still key

Access to trend information is vital as part of a designer's concept creation, development and refinement process and trend forecasting is an aid to capturing the fashion zeitgeist. It is true that many retailers and brands use the similar sources of concept and trend forecasting information as part of their initial development process. This may lead to a certain amount of homogenization in high-street stores and malls around the world, but the key for designers here is interpretation: ensuring that the key messages of the brand remain at the forefront of the product development process. It is vital to retain the design philosophy and brand integrity of individual fashion retailers. If trend information is analysed, interpreted and reproduced in line with a company's strategy then it should help them create the right looks and direction for the business. It is important to note that trend forecasting services and agencies are only as good as the designers and design teams who use them.

Chapter 1 summary

This chapter has dealt with the idea and concept development stage of the fashion business. We have discussed the initial planning stages and data gathering and have learned that there are different types of designers and retailers trying to cater to different customers' tastes and budgets. We have seen that concept and trend forecasting are part of the ingredients required to develop a vision and formalize the design strategy in the fashion business.

Questions and discussion points

We have discussed the ways in which the industry develops its ideas. With this in mind consider the following questions:

1. What do you think are the current macro-level influences affecting the fashion business as a whole? Are any of these mega or micro trends?

2. Which design houses and couture designers do you think are currently influential to the fashion industry as a whole? Explain why.

3. How do mass-market retailers develop original fashion clothing without being accused of copying?

4. What are the different ways in which information can be gathered to create trends and forecast the fashion of the future?

5. How do you think the media and celebrities influence high-street fashion?

6. Which magazines and press do you notice that cover catwalk collections in detail?

7. Write a list of the different ways in which ideas and directions for fashion clothing may be developed.

Exercises

Designers working on the high street have to pay the same attention to detail and channel their creativity just as much as those working in the couture houses. It is equally challenging to design a range of dresses to retail at under $100 (£60) as it is to design a bespoke piece for a client who desires an original item. These exercises are designed to help you channel your own creative thinking.

1. Write a list of 20 different fashion brands or retailers. Now decide if you like or dislike these brands and give the reasons for each of your decisions.

2. Develop a trend or mood board using magazine clippings. Focus on directions in both colour and style. Brainstorm various themes based upon your research.

3. Visit three different fashion retailers of your choice: one department store, one chain store and one designer store. What differences or similarities do you see? Consider style, colour, fabric and trims and compare price points. Analyse all these factors.

4. Visit a current art gallery or museum exhibition. View the exhibits, bearing in mind one or two designer brands that you admire. Then take inspiration from the exhibits to:

a. Think about how some of the information you see may be used in order to help develop inspiration for the brand.

b. Review textile and yarn direction websites online and select fabrics that may inform a collection based on the exhibits, which are in keeping with the philosophy of the brand(s) you admire.

c. Put a colour palette together for next season based on those exhibits that you find most interesting.

1

PRODUCT DEVELOPMENT

2

The product development process is essential to the fashion business. In its broadest sense, the term product development is used to describe the translation of fashion design concepts, ideas and trends into commercial products. The process begins directly after the design team have broken down initial concepts and trends into theme, colour and fabric stories. The next stage is to focus these stories further into specific categories of fashion products and to develop these concepts by turning them into prototype sample garments for review. This chapter examines a generic product development process by identifying the steps followed by high-street and mass-market fashion brands, although each fashion retailer will have its own version of the development process, adapted to its target market and customers.

1 FABRIC SOURCING AT
   PREMIÈRE VISION

The product development
process begins with breaking
down initial concepts and
trends into theme, colour and
fabric stories.

The role of design in business

Different retailers will either elect to buy branded products or develop own-label products; the larger retailers tend to have a mixture of the two. It is important to distinguish between these strategies for the purposes of range planning, which we discuss in more detail later in the chapter.

The designer has a crucial role to develop the right products at the right price. It is essential that fashion retailers employ and train designers with the ability to understand the advantages of adding value at the product development stages. This applies to all segments of the market. It is equally important to be prepared to change the process and adapt it to the ever-changing nature of the market. Designers should have the ability and confidence to interact with buyers and merchandisers and be capable of using appropriate skills to justify their ideas for design direction and trends – this is a key dynamic in the fashion retailing sector.

Private label product development

An important part of a retailer's range planning and design strategy is the continuous development of its own brands, often referred to as 'private label'. This kind of product development grew from the need for retailers to buy exactly what they required for their customers and market.

Own-label product development and fashion design has grown to such an extent that sub-brands and designer labels are now included in this category, all of which are still owned completely by the retailer. Some examples of these are Designers at Debenhams, which incorporates ranges by Betty Jackson, Jasper Conran and John Rocha; and Marks & Spencer sub-brands Autograph, Limited Collection, Per Una, Blue Harbour and Ceriso. Retailers are increasingly collaborating with designers, such as Lanvin, Sonia Rykiel and Karl Lagerfeld at H&M and Alexander McQueen at Target.

1   ALEXANDER MCQUEEN AT TARGET

Retailers are increasingly collaborating with established designers for one-off or ongoing collections; this range is by Alexander McQueen for budget retailer Target.

1

The role of design in business

Brands that are brought in as part of a retail range planning strategy are often intended to 'fit' around the core customer and complement retailers' own labels as a part of the product mix. The trend in the last decade has been for retailers to increase the proportion of own-label fashion brands, driven by the need to retain control of the design and development process. All this means that the retailer's product development resource is now extensive and highly skilled, and less likely to rely on the design capability from suppliers. Nowadays, large teams of designers, technologists and support staff, such as pattern cutters, graphics or print designers and administrators, are employed by fashion retailers to design and develop unique, exclusive ranges.

Developing initial concepts

During the initial concept phase, designers begin by creating black-and-white sketches showing detailed silhouettes to illustrate the garments in their range. These sketches can be created manually with pen and scanned into a CAD program or created directly using CAD software. The initial sketches are used to begin to shape the number of looks or styles in each story for the presentations to buyers.

Mood boards are used to provide an early visual indication of proposed colour direction, fabric and trims and key silhouettes for each look. As well as swatches of fabric, the fashion press will be scanned for ideas and clippings to illustrate the boards. In this way, the contents of international publications such as *Vogue* or *Harper's Bazaar* form part of the planning process for each season.

These boards and the sketches are reviewed, changed and adapted many times in order to determine the exact direction for the brand or retailer. The final process of range planning will result in full colour sketches showing all styles and suggested colours and fabrics. Often referred to as 'ways', each style will have a detailed id or blueprint and description, which will include full working technical drawings known as garment specification sheets or specs.

'Different levels of success have been experienced by these [private label] retailers and the main advantages and reasons for this type of design and product development include store image and loyalty; competitive edge and turnover; higher profits and better margins.'
McGoldrick, 2002

Developing the range plan

After the initial design concept of fabrics, colour and general styling direction have been analysed, the design, buying and merchandising teams begin the next key stage in the process: range planning. This involves turning the rough ideas and sketches into 'stories' or mini collections. There will usually be several general colour and print themes that may be developed simultaneously.

In the range plan the sketches and swatches are grouped together and given names such as 'Bohemian' or 'Nautical' to identify the inspiration and seasonal element. Within each seasonal range there may be up to 12 mini collections or ranges as part of the early stages.

These themed planning boards – which include detailed sketches, as well as colour and fabric at this stage – are used to demonstrate the thought process and direction that the designers believe should be followed for the coming seasons.

'Fashion essentially involves change defined as short-term trends or fads. The competitive ethos of fashion revolves around seasonality. The industry has a vested interest in developing new products for the customer at the expense of existing items: this process is known as planned obsolescence.'
Easey, 2002

The product mix

Fashion retailers are now increasing the number of collections available during a typical season. Pioneered by companies such as Benetton and Zara, the model in fashion retailing has shifted from seasonal purchasing to shorter, rapid bursts of new products. What we know as fast fashion has evolved from the 'quick response' clothing manufacturing model (which we discuss in more detail in chapter 4, the supply chain). The buyers and merchandisers will review with the design teams the previous season's sales history, such as good and bad sellers, emerging trends and the performance of their competition in the market. This is often referred to as a 'lessons learnt' stage and it is a crucial part of the range planning process.

The product mix and range planning process is loosely based upon what is known as the marketing mix (or the seven Ps), which is the total offer to customers (see the diagram, right). Each fashion retailer will adapt these principles to suit their brand in the context of its market. The marketing mix is a useful model to explain the key stages within fashion retail. This chapter will focus upon product development so we will examine this first and return to the others in subsequent chapters.

The range plan

The range plan is essential for determining product mix. The plan contains complete detail of all styles, including the required lead times for each style and how many phases are going to exist within each range. The overall styling direction and theme of each range will usually be determined at this stage. Within a season phases are timed for each collection, which allows new colour statements and products to be introduced.

The team of designers, buyers and merchandisers will determine the total number of styles required per category of product, such as knitwear or tailoring. They will analyse the proportion and balance of each range, such as quantity of tops versus trousers or daywear versus evening wear (usually there will be more tops than bottoms and more daywear than occasion wear). They will also decide what percentage of each range will be fashion, classic or basics. Finally, they make decisions on types of fabrics and numbers of colours per style, based on trends, availability and suitability. Additionally, the size ranges will be agreed at this stage, such as skirt and trouser lengths for example, or special fits such as petite or tall.

'The initial stages of developing a seasonal range typically occur a full year before it starts to appear in the shops. Retailers have introduced 3–5 phases within the season, typically lasting on average 8–12 weeks each. This trend of mid-season purchasing is changing the traditional two-season fashion regime and having far-reaching effects upon buyer–supplier relationships.'
Tyler, Heeley & Bhamra, 2006

PLACE
- × MULTI-CHANNEL
- × WHOLESALE
- × LOCAL-EXPORT
- × INTERNET

PRODUCT
- × DESIGN TECHNOLOGY
- × USABILITY
- × USEFULNESS
- × VALUE
- × QUALITY
- × BRAND
- × WARRANTY

PRICE
- × PENETRATION STRATEGY
- × COST-PLUS
- × LOSS LEADER
- × MORE

TARGET MARKET

PHYSICAL EVIDENCE
- × USER STORIES
- × RECOMMENDATIONS
- × OFFICE PREMISES
- × BUZZ

PROMOTION
- × ADVERTISING
- × RECOMMENDATIONS
- × SPECIAL OFFERS
- × USER TESTING

PROCESS
- × SERVICE DELIVERY
- × COMPLAINTS
- × RESPONSE TIME

PEOPLE
- × FOUNDERS
- × EMPLOYEES
- × CULTURE
- × CUSTOMER SERVICE

1

1   THE SEVEN PS

The four Ps (product, price,
place and promotion) were
established by Borden in
1965. The model was further
extended, known as the
extended marketing
mix, to include three
intangible, service-related
elements: people, process
and physical evidence.

The product mix

1

The product mix: basics or core items

Hosiery, T-shirts, denim and lingerie are all examples of basic or core items. It is important to note that these require redesigning and continual seasonal updates, which may include new fabrics, improved fit, colour and new trimmings to coordinate with the fashion look.

There will also be key pieces or must-haves that are added to the basics range each season. The basic product lines are usually safe and best-selling items and must be available all year round, regardless of the season. These are mass market, high volume lines. There is a higher margin than for fashion items and a low product development cost.

The product mix: fashion items

These are the true 'fashion' lines, which demand crucial timing and very limited selling periods. It is impossible to list them here as they are simply 'fashion' and therefore unpredictable. However, it is important to note that garments that are fashion items may in the future become basics or classics, such as the little black dress.

Different product categories have different requirements; for example, in some ranges there must be more basics available as well as fashion items. The balance of each product, phase and range is crucial to the success of product development translation from the design concepts.

2

1+2 RANGE PLANNING

The range planning process usually involves a collaboration of the designer, buyer and merchandiser to determine the product mix. This establishes the design details of all styles, the required lead times for each style and the number of phases within each range.

3 THE PRODUCT MIX: BASICS

Basic product lines are best-selling, high-volume items that are available all year round, regardless of the season.

3

Garment specifications: sampling

Once the range-planned styles have been agreed and signed off, the design team will work with the pattern technologists and fabric technologists to perfect the detailed information required in order to proceed to the initial sampling stages.

The garment spec is sent to the relevant manufacturer with clear instructions on how it should look and the type of fabric required for making the sample. A CAD (computer-aided design) sketch and diagram or photograph will be included, along with a mock-up or **toile** of part, or all, of the entire garment. It is usually dependent upon the size of the company whether or not it has its own sample room facilities. Making samples is an expensive and laborious part of the design process and each sample will take far longer to make than its mass-produced final version. This is why the range planning process is so crucial: it is far cheaper and more efficient for retailers and their suppliers to develop mood boards and sketches than excessive sampling of garments.

Many large retailers now rely heavily on their suppliers to perfect and develop buying samples for them. These days, CAD techniques are used to enable design and buying teams to view multiple colourways and detailing of garments without the need to sample them all; however, it is important to note that this relies on the CAD operator having good communication and design skills.

1

1   SAMPLING PROCESS

Garment sampling may occur
in-house, depending on the
size of the fashion retailer;
often the retailer will rely on
its manufacturers and suppliers.

Toile

A toile is a mock-up used
to check the pattern
and design of a garment.
Different to a sample, it is
used at an earlier stage
in the design process.
The toile may be made in
calico or a cheaper version
of the required fabric.

Garment specifications: sampling

Performance testing

All products developed must pass performance testing requirements. It is usually the responsibility of the supplier to ensure that all products meet, or exceed, the standards required by the retailer. Before finalizing or signing an agreement, it is important that suppliers understand and agree the quality-standard requirements of the retailer. It is normal practice to have both fabric and garments tested before the product is delivered; typically, the testing is done at a third-party testing facility such as Intertek or ITS. At times, the buyers and design team will designate the testing lab. Sometimes the retailer (or buyer) will submit the garments for testing; however, often the buyer will require that the supplier submits the fabric and garments directly to the testing laboratory and then provide them with copies of the test results. Final bulk testing is completed before bulk production of garments commences. Accurate records must be kept by the manufacturer and the retailer in case of any faults or customer complaints. Many retailers also undertake surprise testing on garments after they arrive into the stores. This technique is used to discourage suppliers from submitting garments in bulk that do not match up to the quality approved for final production.

'Successful fashion design in commercial terms is based upon providing what customers want frequently before they realize it. In fashion retailing successful design equals sales. If a garment design sells well, the basic shape will be "milked" and reworked in a variety of fabrics and colours and prints.'
Jackson and Shaw, 2005

1

Specialist fabrics

Some garments will require additional
testing, such as items that claim to be flame
retardant, water resistant, anti-bacterial
and so on. So-called 'smart' fabrics are used
for sport and other performance activities,
which need to be fit for purpose; Teflon-coated,
breathable and water-repellent fabrics
require rigorous testing before use.
Even simple products, such as a T-shirt
jersey, for example, require certain dye
stuffs to withstand washing and to limit the
shrinkage of fabric. Children's apparel
requires additional product safety testing.

1 GARMENT SAMPLING

By the time it reaches the mass-
production stage, each garment
style will have been technically
engineered in order to be as
cost-effective and aesthetically
pleasing as possible, reflecting
the original model and ideas of
the designer.

Interview: George Sharp

GEORGE SHARP

1980–1983

studied at Manchester Polytechnic (now MMU), graduating with a BA in fashion design

1983

in his final year in college, Sharp launched his brand Armstrong Collins Sharp, sold in upscale stores in London and his own freestanding store in Manchester

1984–2000

held various design positions at Bellville Sassoon, with involvement in fabric development and research, concept development and design, illustration, fitting and checking of garments and the selling and styling of the final collections

2001–2007

head of design at Escada, German fashion house based in Munich

2008–2009

Vice President of design at Ellen Tracy, New York

2009–present

creative director of St John Knits, a premier brand renowned for innovative knits

Who is the typical St John Knits customer?

 The St John customer is a 40+ sophisticated, elegant woman, who is successful and confident. She loves fashion, but chooses trends carefully; she never wants clothes to be costumey. She prefers understatement with subtle and refined details to anything too obvious or too literal. But she loves colours, prints, luxurious fabrics and impeccable fit. She is more about 'stealth wealth' than conspicuous consumption.

 Please introduce us to St John Knits

 St John Knits is one of the premier names in American fashion. It was founded in 1962 by Robert and Marie Gray and has evolved from a small family operation to the global luxury brand known today. The company is headquartered in Irvine, California, employs approximately 3,000 people and operates dozens of offices and manufacturing facilities worldwide. St John Knits is today as it has always been, a carefully managed company, maintaining consistency of product throughout the design and manufacturing process.

'Our customers don't like clothes that scream out a label. They just like people to think they're well dressed.'

Interview: George Sharp

Q How do you try to keep customer loyalty whilst introducing new looks into the brand?

A I go with my gut instinct (and we have to take calculated risks on design and trends) but I don't take a traditional route of following trends slavishly as I think that, once again, it is about knowing the customers. First thought equals the best thought usually when designing and developing the collections. With St John we have created timeless investment pieces that are very neutral in colour tones, with some other highlights in touches like a blouse, a sweater or a scarf.

Q What is your design and style philosophy?

A I'm a classicist and am happy to see the fashion pendulum swinging back in that direction. It looks so new and right to see a woman in a crisp white shirt and a great pair of pants or in a cashmere top belted over a perfectly fitting skirt.

St John's design philosophy has always reflected my aesthetics: it is renowned for its great American knitwear. I like clean, modern clothes for real women. Creating clothes is not just about runway shows.

Q What is great style in your view?

A Great style is definitely about confidence! Style comes from the confidence and comfort of wearing what you know looks best on you; it's making a look your own – not about slavishly following trends.

Those who do not try too hard and edit brands to suit them will look good; it is more important now that a woman's wardrobe works hard and is right for them.

Q Which other designers
do you admire?

A I'm a huge fan of the fashion
designer Yohji Yamamoto.
His work is incredible.
And I admire Tom Ford:
he made fashion sexy
and inspirational because
he was not afraid to be
commercial. Commercial
is not a dirty word. I love
commercial.

Q Which commercial mass-
market retailers do you
regard as doing a good job
with product development?

A On the high street I would
say that Uniqlo is doing
a great job with quality
products and style. The Jil
Sander range mixed with
the Japanese philosophy
has created great products –
they definitely have the cool
factor.

I have to say that the UK
probably has better high-
street retailers than the
USA. Here we have so
many bridge line ranges:
all designer names such
as Ellen Tracy, Adrienne
Vittadini, Dana Buchman
and Ann Klein – these
are the US equivalent of
high-street brands.

Q Where does your main
source of inspiration
come from?

A My greatest sources of
inspiration are my wife and
friends. My wife is a stylist
and has an amazing eye.

'We track the customer very well with the help
of the retailers such as Nordstrom and Neiman
Marcus; they tell us what she is spending money
on and what she is not spending it on.'

Interview: George Sharp

Q **What are your thoughts on range planning and buying?**

A Years ago the great buyers were great merchants – they did not buy off a range plan or spreadsheet.

Unfortunately now, too many buyers lack the experience to buy instinctively. It is often the case that they will become too focused upon what I call 'rear view mirror' thinking and end up making decisions based purely on the previous season's sales. I advise buyers that they should not over-analyse the products but edit the collections and buy with confidence from the ranges.

Be passionate about the product and use that instinct to buy well. I don't believe in themes, it is about having the right fabrics, colour and style for your customers. We need to stay one step ahead of our customer, to give her something new that she does not know that she wants. The biggest competition we have is from the customer's own closet!

Q **How do you research your customers?**

A I am totally against so-called 'market research' into fashion customers per se. It's fine if you are analysing the sales of frozen peas and washing machines but we, the designers, have to set the tone for the customers with the products. You have to challenge the customers, meet them, get out to stores and keep the customer engaged; to find out about her lifestyle and see how far you can push the product boundaries.

Customers do not have time to fill in questionnaires and designers need to go with their creative instincts, in terms of product development.

'The most important thing for a designer is to really know your customer.'

Q **What is a typical day for you in the design studio?**

A I always get in to the office early enough to check my mail and diary then have coffee before things get too hectic! It is different from anywhere else that I have worked. Glenn McMahon (the CEO) gives me a free rein and is very product-aware. I find it's a great environment to work and design in.

We create fabulous knitwear, which means technically we have to work around a year or so ahead creating our own fabrics. Creating fabrics and knits I find is a great challenge; with knitwear it's one step further back in product development, starting with the yarn.

I am very hands-on with product and whatever else I am doing and I do get involved in everything including design, styling, PR, marketing, sales and strategy. You would expect anyone in a similarly senior position to be involved in the key decision-making processes in the business.

I think it is essential for designers to be 'marketing savvy' and confident enough to go out and meet the customers. You need to be able to sell it as well as design it! I remain passionate about the product and everything that I do with the brand.

Q **What advice would you give to would-be designers or product developers?**

A Don't start your own business straight out of college like I did; you will not have the knowledge!

Work for a fashion business and understand all aspects of it, like sales, finance, merchandising and manufacturing. You need to know how it all works as without it you cannot be taken seriously.

When you leave college you may think you know it all but that's when the hard work and learning all really starts.

Case study: Marks & Spencer

Marks & Spencer (M&S) is possibly the best-known UK clothing retailer and its place in retailing history has been well documented. It began by trading as a market stall in Leeds, England and became a limited company in 1926. It created its unique position in the market by emphasizing quality, innovation and excellent value for money. Historically, M&S developed its fashion products in conjunction with its suppliers and manufacturers and relied upon large-scale design briefing input from its own buying teams.

M&S grew into an institution as an iconic fashion retailer in the UK with over 370 stores. It revolutionized the high street with its pioneering and good quality own-label fashion, built upon an innovative approach to design, buying and merchandising.

Going into decline

Unfortunately, by the 1990s, M&S found itself with an excess of suppliers, high-product costs and an unattractive and fragmented product range. The arrival of fast fashion and discount retailers in the UK changed the face of high-street fashion, by offering greater choice for consumers and in turn creating a more difficult and less certain environment for the traditional retailers. M&S had gradually become a casualty of this environment by steadfastly refusing to change its product process or its people. In what was an increasingly fast-moving retail environment, M&S continued to decline until it reached crisis point, only producing two to three collections per year. This, in addition to a complete lack of advertising, meant that sales plummeted. Customers began to shop elsewhere, favouring retailers that sold cheap, disposable fashion, with many new collections arriving on a continuous basis.

'A beacon of light in UK manufacturing.'
Bevan, 2007

RETAIL STRATEGY

For years Marks & Spencer used no form of advertising nor did it have a marketing director; it created its unique position in the market by emphasizing quality, innovation and excellent value for money.

'There was no handwriting; it was a mixture of everyone's influences bundled together. In the end we had nothing that was appealing.'
Marks & Spencer

New product development

Sir Stuart Rose was appointed CEO in 2004 and he helped turn it around after its rocky ten-year period. Following his appointment Rose swiftly recruited marketing director Steven Sharp and Kate Bostock as head of womenswear.

Together Sharp, Rose and Bostock set about transforming product development, the buying and merchandising functions and the decision-making process. This new team, together with the in-house buyers and designers, began by identifying the target customer: who she was, where she shopped and what her aspirations were. They identified a core group of average- to middle-income women who worked full-time, had children and were short of time.

The next step was to adapt the supply chain model. Against a backdrop of competition whose stores had new styles arriving every two to four weeks, M&S was slow off the mark to spot new trends and make them available to customers. Stuart Rose and his buying team introduced a quick response supply chain model: taking risks on products, manufacturing close to home in Turkey or Eastern Europe, and keeping fabric in stock to make quick repeats.

The third crucial step was to invest in advertising. It began a huge advertising campaign using some big names including British icon Twiggy, the 1960s model, who identified with the core womenswear customer. Some of the first, newly designed fashion items were modelled by Twiggy and featured on TV and in magazines. Any items modelled by Twiggy (including a certain beige draped cardigan, now referred to as 'the cardigan that saved M&S'), quickly began to sell out.

Case study: Marks & Spencer

Product development strategy: direct sourcing

At M&S the buyers are the ones holding the power in product development – over 50 designers are employed at its HQ. All M&S design and buying teams issue very clear briefings to their manufacturers and, whilst there are now many suppliers around the globe, M&S retains control by closely monitoring the process and specifying in detail its requirements for each style. Initiated in the last few years in order to improve speed to market specifically on fast fashion lines, M&S follows a 'direct buying' process, which involves design and buying teams working directly with suppliers at source of manufacture, without using any middlemen or agents. This type of direct sourcing enables a quicker and more cost-effective procurement process: it can help with the availability of raw materials; technical qualities of fibres and fabrics; fabric construction and innovation; and value analysis.

In order to directly source textiles and undertake design and product development, teams at M&S need to understand the technical characteristics of particular fabrics, and how these may affect the general appeal of its fashion ranges. Within each buying department, the buyers, merchandisers, designers and technologists work together to formulate each range focusing upon an area of expertise. Sourcing managers work closely with key suppliers to develop relationships. They employ staff previously employed by suppliers, which has an added competitive advantage as the knowledge of fabric and garment quality has been transferred to the retailer.

PRODUCT DEVELOPMENT

The buying process at M&S, as pioneered by Simon Marks in the 1950s, has evolved over the years. Its design and buying teams today issue clear briefs to the manufacturers and retain control by closely monitoring the process.

Innovation at M&S

M&S pioneered its private-label fashion by analysing trends and developing innovative and fashionable products, such as machine-washable suits, wool and cashmere knitwear, at affordable prices.

It creates the type of product today just as in the past that 'it cannot find elsewhere yet knows it can sell' (Bevan, 2008). This is the essence of private label product development in fashion retailing. There is now much less proliferation of similar products, such as many types of black trousers, for example; these have been replaced by key shapes in fashionable, innovative fabrics offering real choice to the customer.

In addition, M&S has implemented the Walmart 'good, better and best' price matrix system in order to adjust the price of its clothing. It has redesigned and repositioned its product, price and market position to align with that of its competition. M&S has successfully completed its repositioning strategy whilst maintaining the core values of providing quality, innovation and good value for customers.

'Formal innovation is a change in the product form not necessarily associated with changes in product functions and product process. Formal innovation is decisive in productive fields as those of fashion and design goods... here, innovation depends much less on engineering factors, as for technological innovation, and much more on intangible factors, such as aesthetics, imagination and taste, close relatives of artistic creativity.'
Bianchi and Borlotti, 1996

Chapter 2 summary

This chapter has explored the concept of product development within a fashion retail business and the process of range planning. We have seen that most large-scale retailers and high-street brands develop ranges in-house in order to control the process. In addition, we have discussed how retailers develop the product and marketing mix to suit their customers' needs and to stay ahead of the competition.

Questions and discussion points

We have examined the generic product development process and the process of range planning. Consider the following questions in connection with fashion retail and your understanding of chapter two:

1. Identify the different types of products in similar categories from different fashion retail stores – try to ascertain bought-in brands and own labels. What key differences do you see?

2. Which retailers that develop own labels /ranges /lines do you regard as fashionable? Explain why.

3. How well do you think big chain stores are at presenting the key trends to customers? Discuss.

4. Which fashion brands do you perceive as being innovative and which do you see as not?

5. How well do you think fashion retailers are interpreting catwalk and general trends? Which fashion retailers do you perceive as doing this most effectively?

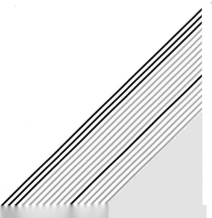

Exercises

Fashion retailers spend a great deal of time range planning, which is not always obvious to the public at large. Take some time to examine a variety of fashion retailers and the products on offer. These exercises are designed to make you think like a commercial designer or fashion buyer and understand this key part in the process.

1. Visit a fashion retailer of your own choice and identify how many colour stories or themes are currently in stock. What do you think is the specific design direction and overall styling theme of each range? Review the number of styles on display and identify different types of products that you consider to be core, fashion or key items.

2. Think about a key trend that you have identified and consider how different fashion retailers or fashion brands have interpreted this. Compare and contrast retailers' own brands and review key differences or similarities.

3. Take a close look at fabric and detail: what are the emerging themes that you see from retailer to retailer?

   Examine fabric construction and washing instructions in a variety of stores; again, do these vary by retailer or brand?

4. Develop your understanding of technical innovation within fashion retail. Visit a sportswear retailer and identify some smart breathable or specially finished products and identify any promotional swing tags that explain the key benefits to customers.

1

RETAIL STRATEGY

3

Shopping, or 'retail therapy', is a recognizable global leisure activity. Retailers compete with each other by creating interesting and exciting shopping and leisure environments dedicated to attracting and retaining customers. Additionally, the advent of e-tailing and multi-channel retail formats has increased the dynamic and complex ways in which fashion clothing is sold and promoted to the public at large. In chapter two we discussed product, one of the seven Ps of the marketing mix (see page 46). This chapter reviews position, place, price and people as part of retail strategy. It explores the strategies used by retailers to deliver clothing to customers across different retail formats.

1 REPUBLIC RETAIL STORE

Fashion retailing is one of the world's largest business sectors and the mega retailers continue to expand globally. All retailers must have a strategy that encompasses the philosophy of the company or brand, in order to present the product offer in the most effective way, using the most suitable and efficient retail formats available to attract and inspire customers.

Defining retail strategy

Johnson and Scholes define strategy as 'the direction and scope of an organization over the long-term: which achieves advantage for the organization through its configuration of resources within a challenging environment, to meet the needs of markets and to fulfil stakeholder expectations.'

There are two major components to marketing and retail strategy: how the business will address the increasingly competitive marketplace; and how it intends to implement and support its day-to-day operations. It is essential to identify the main competition and to understand strengths and weaknesses alongside those of the competition, which will help to determine retail strategy and position in the market. It is also essential to analyse the business, its competitors and the external environment: **macro factors** can positively or negatively impact the industry and the market growth potential of the product or service.
In addition, key components for strategic analysis include a review of product, price, market position, strength and predictability. A regular review of the strength and viability of fashion products and the provision of customer service development programmes will heavily influence the direction of any retail strategy.

1 THE FIVE FORCES MODEL

In his book *Competitive Advantage* Michael Porter developed the Five Forces framework as a technique for understanding and examining the level of power and competitiveness in business. It is a useful tool for analysing the competition.

PORTER'S FIVE FORCES ANALYSIS

1

Macro factors

Macro factors are wider, external forces; a good example of a macro factor is an economic recession, which has a negative impact upon consumer spending and behaviour in general.

2 SWOT

SWOT stands for strengths, weaknesses, opportunities and threats. An honest appraisal of the strengths and weaknesses of the fashion business is a critical factor in the development of its retail strategy.

STRENGTHS
BRAND REPUTATION; LOYAL CUSTOMER BASE; PROPRIETARY KNOWLEDGE; COMPETITIVE SOURCES OF RAW MATERIALS; TALENTED LABOUR FORCE; INDUSTRIAL ADVANTAGES; TRADE CONNECTIONS

WEAKNESSES
NEW DESIGNERS WITH NO REPUTATION; LACK OF NAME; NEW LINE WITHOUT A FOLLOWING; COSTLY LABOUR FORCE

THREATS
SHIFTING TRENDS; RECESSION; TRADE BARRIERS; GOVERNMENT REGULATIONS

OPPORTUNITIES
EMERGING MARKETS; TECHNOLOGICAL ADVANCES; REMOVAL OF INTERNATIONAL TRADE BARRIERS; NEW LABOUR FORCE

2

Defining retail strategy

1 PESTEL DIAGRAM

There are many factors in the macro-environment that will affect the decision-making process within any industry. To help analyse these factors, retailers can categorize them using the PESTEL model, which is a useful tool in retail strategy.

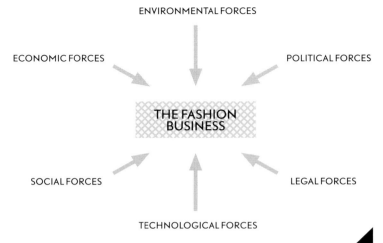

ENVIRONMENTAL FORCES

ECONOMIC FORCES

POLITICAL FORCES

THE FASHION BUSINESS

SOCIAL FORCES

LEGAL FORCES

TECHNOLOGICAL FORCES

1

PESTEL framework

We looked at the PESTEL framework in chapter 1 (see page 22) in the context of trends and forecasting. Retailers also use this model to analyse their environment and competition.

Political: this could be a country introducing changes to import duty.

Economic: recession or boom can affect spending.

Sociological: longer life expectancy means an older population, which in turn affects the products required.

Technological: customer demand for instant information means an increase in the use of marketing tools such as social media.

Environmental: an eco or green and organic movement in textiles.

Legal: changes in copyright law can influence fashion retailers' ability to manufacture certain products.

Implementing retail strategy

Every retail strategy must engage with the philosophy of the company or brand. From retail strategy a fashion business will develop a marketing strategy or plan in order to present the offer in the most effective way and by using the most suitable and efficient retail formats available. It is the brand 'DNA', which is captured in the shopping experience to attract and inspire customers.

Today's consumer is offered so much choice; as such, the combination of new and innovative store environments and great products is vital to ensure a successful retail strategy. Implementing strategy requires continual review and benchmarking against the competition and analysis of the market environment whilst ensuring that it responds to customers' requirements.

2

Porter's strategies

Porter (1986) identified three generic strategies that can be used to identify the type of retail strategy implemented across different fashion businesses. Each retail strategy is concerned with creating competitive advantage within market position.

× Overall cost leadership. Low-cost, high-volume retailers tend to follow this strategy, for example Primark, Forever 21 and Target. Companies such as this rely on cost leadership for competitive advantage.

× Differentiation. Variety and department stores are experts in brand layering and differentiation within their ranges to attract different parts of the market.

× Focus. This is very much a niche market strategy, focusing on one particular product or category. Luxury brands use focus strategy, for example Louis Vuitton and Hermès.

2 PRIMARK RETAIL STRATEGY

UK retailer Primark satisfies customer needs by providing low-cost, high-volume goods in such a way as to differentiate itself from the competition. This combination of cost leadership and differentiation is a major contributor to its success in maintaining competitive advantage.

'If you look at the best retailers out there they are constantly reinventing themselves.'
Burnes, 2009

The marketing mix: position

1

Fashion retailing is a dynamic and fluid business and strategy needs to reflect this: creating a competitive advantage in a market sector is an essential part of maintaining the necessary level of interest.

Economies of scale

The term 'economies of scale' is used to refer to the fall in the average cost per unit as the scale of output (such as the size of the company or its manufacturing capabilities) increases.

Identifying market position enables a company to determine its strategy and direction in order to present and maintain a strong recognizable brand image and identity to customers. Analysis of market position involves a lot of detail, such as cost control, infrastructure, cost of materials, **economies of scale**, management skills, availability of personnel and compatibility of manufacturing resources. A fashion retailing strategy should highlight the way in which the business may construct entry barriers to the competition. These can include high switching costs, gaining substantial benefit from economies of scale via sourcing policies; creating exclusive access to distribution channels to prevent others from using them; and the ability to clearly differentiate products. This is linked to the retailer's ability to buy in bulk and volume and to work with suppliers effectively to create advantages.

'It is the strength of our operating model that allows New Look to capitalize on fashion trends. We try to avoid both a strongly fashion-forward positioning (attempting to predict fashion trends before they take hold) and that of a fashion follower (with the risk that momentum for a trend has passed by the time the buying team has reacted). Instead, we seek to operate at the "crest of the fashion wave". This means that our buying team will identify when fashion trends have gained some momentum, and then react quickly through our flexible supply chain in order to deliver significant volume of products reflecting those trends to the market.'

New Look

1   RETAIL POSITION

Today's customers have a huge amount of choice; it is vital for a fashion business to identify and maintain market position as part of its retail strategy.

Another important factor to consider is the longevity of fashion products and market position. This is determined by the potential for competitive imitation, the ability to maintain high or low prices and the potential to plan for inevitable fashion product **obsolescence**. Crucial as part of its competitiveness and positioning is the financial viability and profitability of the business. This will enable it to take key risks and make critical business decisions without too much influence from investors, suppliers and banks.

Obsolescence

An object, service or practice that is no longer wanted goes through the state of obsolescence; it applies to anything that goes 'out of fashion'. According to Mike Easey, the development process for 'the apparel products associated with frequent changes in customer lifestyle and requirements, and that highly rely on fashion marketing, is considered as a planned obsolescence' (Easey, 2002).

The marketing mix: place

Competition has never been fiercer in international fashion retail, yet there are more opportunities than ever for fashion retailers to obtain and keep new customers. Thanks to the Internet, customers can now shop 24/7 if they wish. It is this complexity and dynamism that keeps fashion businesses moving and evolving, much like fashion itself. In addition to retail format, the retailer's location adds another dimension to the marketing offer.

Some retailers will own or rent their own stores whilst others will use different methods to expand strategy and create the most appropriate and interesting retail formats. Many fashion retailers are now using a multi-channel retail strategy to create brand equity. There has been an increase in the number of innovative retail formats, such as pop-up shops and members-only discount e-tailing.

Concessions

Often referred to as a 'shop within a shop', concessions are generally located within large department or variety stores. Many designer brands will use this retail method. One retailer is effectively leasing space to another, which can be a flexible way of testing the market and making use of the retailer's buying and selling expertise. It also means lower investment for the brand and there are potentially higher levels of customer **footfall**.

Footfall

The number of people visiting a shop or a chain of shops in a period of time is called its footfall. It is an indicator of the reach a retailer has, but it needs to be converted into sales and this is not guaranteed to happen. Many retailers have struggled to turn high footfall into sales.

1 DEBENHAMS

Many fashion retailers now use a variety of formats to create brand equity. UK retailer Debenhams has a portfolio of 55 own brands as well as international brands that are either bought in or available through in-store concessions. The retailer has over 140 stores across the UK and a further 35 international franchise stores.

1

The marketing mix: place

Franchises

A franchise strategy is often used by retailers who wish to internationalize because it involves low investment: the franchisee has the relevant local knowledge and invests in buying the stock, staffing the store and paying the rent. It means the franchisee can trade under a recognizable, well-known brand and benefit from national or international advertising campaigns. This strategy is often used by so-called niche retailers, such as the Body Shop, Tie Rack and Accessorize.

Licensing

A good way for a brand to promote and expand is by selling licences to use its brand name and manufacture products; it is a market penetration technique used by many designer brands. However, it is important to monitor and police the products to ensure they remain true to the brand image. Burberry famously fell foul of over-licensing its products, most notably in Asia, and had to then carry out a costly and time-consuming repositioning strategy.

Online retail

Advances in technology have contributed to the huge growth in online retail, which enables consumers to shop 24/7. The advent of e-tailing has enabled brands to establish a global presence and create yet another competitive edge, a strategy that many fashion brands are now striving for in order to grow market share and increase brand equity.

Designer outlets

In recent years there has been a big increase in the number of large-scale retail outlets, which originated in the USA and have spread to Europe and Asia. Some of these outlet malls are used by designers to distribute out-of-season goods and excess stock. Brands such as Hugo Boss, Jil Sander, Ralph Lauren and DKNY are just some of the names that use this retail method to generate lucrative sales revenue. UK company McArthurGlen is one of the largest owners and leasing agents of such designer outlets, with a number of entire outlet villages throughout the UK and Europe.

1+2 FRANCHISE OPPORTUNITIES

Franchising can offer more sales opportunities than standalone stores. It is a low-risk, low-investment strategy and a flexible way of testing a market. Accessorize and Levi's both use a franchise strategy within their global expansion programmes.

1

2

An online version of the outlet store is the members-only designer discounter, such as Gilt Groupe, Vente-Privee, Cocosa and Brand Alley. These e-tailers all operate in a similar way, offering virtual sample sales with limited availability. Members are emailed with the latest offers and given a time limit to make purchases. These retail outlets offer a safety net to brands and designers, enabling them to move excess stock and expensive samples. US company Gilt Groupe saw an opportunity to provide luxury and value to consumers through viral marketing and time-limited sales. It sells newer brands such as Rodarte, Derek Lam and Christian Louboutin. The company has profited during an economic downturn and now has over two million members.

Pop-up shops

Pop-up shops, also known as 'guerilla' stores, have increased in popularity over recent years. The concept of the pop-up store is to trial new or well-known brands within a temporary shop outlet. In times of recession they have proved to be a winning low-risk format for many brands.

'The store and transactional retail website is the image a brand wants to present to the public in order to sell its fashion products. These have been referred to as "retail cathedrals".'
M Tungate, 2006

The marketing mix: place

1 CHINA'S HIGH STREET

China appears to have an almost insatiable appetite for western brands, within the luxury sector as well as high-street names such as Zara, Gap and H&M.

1

Internationalization

Many fashion retailers have become international and many others continually try to create a global presence as a part of long-term strategy.

The most successful retailers and fashion brands maximize global presence through international partnerships, which enable access to local knowledge and an understanding of local culture, language and taste.

New and emerging markets create new customers and enable fashion retailers to expand. Examples of new markets include Brazil, China, Russia and India as well as Eastern Europe and the Middle East. It is widely acknowledged that the Chinese market in particular has matured very quickly. However, it is far from easy to establish a global presence and it may take years to find the correct partner and format. It is essential that fashion retailers who pursue an international strategy first understand the local market and ensure that the offer is relevant. It may be necessary to adapt and change the mix or offer to fit in with regional requirements.

Well-established global brands such as Gap, Nike and H&M have stores around the world, tailoring the product offering and store environment according to the customers and market of each region.

The marketing mix: price

Price is an essential part of retail strategy. A pricing strategy can help to determine the speed at which a company achieves its marketing objectives. A low price strategy is used to build sales via volume, as used by retailers such as Primark in the UK and Forever 21 and Target in the USA. A higher price strategy is used by companies selling high-quality products, such as luxury brand Louis Vuitton. Whatever the strategy, the price levels should be set in conjunction with the type of fashion product and be appropriate to market position.

It is important for retailers to work closely with suppliers and manufacturers in order to establish price and profit margins – the retail selling price (RSP). This will ensure that objectives are achieved and that all parties involved are satisfied: this will, of course, include the customer and the price they are willing to pay, as well as the requirements of the retailer and the supplier. All parties must cover their overheads and make a profit to retain sustainability in the long term.

Most fashion retailers use price promotions, sales and special offers as part of a pricing strategy. These are usually planned in the budget setting process at the start of each season and accounted for by buying and merchandising teams.

1 PRICE MATRIX

Fashion retailers use a price matrix to plan a pricing structure across different levels of products on offer. Penetration pricing involves setting prices artificially low to drum up interest in the product. Price skimming involves charging an unnecessarily high price to create a sense of exclusivity; this strategy is often used when launching a new or innovative product to the market.

LOW · Quality · HIGH

ECONOMY · PENETRATION

Price

SKIMMING · PREMIUM

HIGH

1

2 HIGH PRICE STRATEGY

Luxury brands use a higher price strategy, which is set in conjunction with fashion product type: exclusive, often limited edition, top-quality garments. The pricing strategy should be appropriate to the brand's market position.

2

Price matrix

Different fashion ranges need different price strategies. Products that are referred to as 'opening price point' (OPP) are high in volume and usually low in price. High fashion items, which involve more risk than basic items, will command a higher price and therefore create a wider margin.

An important part of the pricing strategy is to determine customers' spending patterns and average spend per range. It is usual for most fashion brands and retailers to use a price matrix within which they segment ranges into 'good, better and best'. This matrix can help fashion retailers to plan a pricing structure across different levels of fashion products on offer.

The marketing mix: people

1

A key element of a successful retail strategy is its people: those who understand the relevant technologies in the fashion industry and are able to perform the tasks necessary to meet the development objectives of the business. This goes hand in hand with business infrastructure in terms of organization, recruiting capabilities, employee benefit programmes, customer support facilities and its logistical capabilities.

Fashion retailing can be a difficult and volatile business; it requires making quick, risky decisions about fast-moving fashion items. In fashion retailing there are two key roles: the buyers and the merchandisers; these are the people who ensure that the fashion retailer has the right products in the right place at the right time.

The competence of the management team and the 'stars' within it cannot be overlooked: it is important to manage talent within a business. Jane Shepherdson, former brand director at Topshop, contributed a great deal to the retailer's success: updating its ranges, buying more fashionable, trend-led items and launching young designer initiatives. Shepherdson left the company in 2006 to work with ethical brand People Tree and upmarket high-street brand Whistles, both of which are much smaller, independent retailers. Her departure highlights the fact that an over-reliance on key members of staff should be avoided as it can increase risk. There should be some form of succession planning in place as well as good training programmes to enable others to follow suit.

Also part of people management within retail strategy is the retailer's ability to form successful designer collaborations. Topshop and H&M are well-known for their designer ranges – notable examples are Sonia Rykiel and Karl Lagerfeld at H&M and Christopher Kane and Preen at Topshop.

Retail experts

There are a number of internationally renowned business experts and retailers who understand the market and who know how to attract and keep the right talent in terms of design, buying, sourcing and merchandising. Sir Philip Green of Arcadia and Sir Stuart Rose of M&S are great examples of retail experts who are running large-scale, successful fashion organizations; also Millard 'Mickey' Drexler (CEO of J Crew Group and former CEO of Gap) and Angela Ahrendts at Burberry.

Other well-known global fashion business names are Victor Fung (chairman of Li & Fung) and Silas Chou, as well as Kenneth Fang. Although specifically involved in sourcing, these individuals have significant influence over global brands including Pringle and Episode, amongst others.

'It's the graduates who've studied fashion-related degrees that tend to swing towards a buying role.'
Arcadia Group

1 FASHION BUYING

Fashion buyers are expected to be one step ahead of the market, continually seeking out forthcoming trends.

The marketing mix: people

The role of the buyer

Along with the designer, the fashion buyer is crucial to the success of fashion retailing and range planning. As retailers have focused increasingly upon designing and producing their own designs, the importance of the team involved in buying, merchandising, product design and development cannot be emphasized enough. Buyers are expected to be one step ahead of the market and continually seeking out what they refer to as 'newness'. They need to take calculated risks at times with huge budgets but must also recognize the demands and needs of the core customers.

A fashion buyer for a high-street chain such as Topshop or Forever 21 will work with suppliers and in-house design teams to identify and develop the trends for the next season. Buyers for department stores, such as House of Fraser, will work with brands to buy in selected items from a collection, or may work with suppliers to modify a trend that will best suit their target market for their own brands. The buyer must have a good eye for fashion with a keen business sense. A common misconception is that a buying role is design-led. While there are elements of creativity, the most important skill is to think commercially because, ultimately, the items must sell well.

Fashion buying as a career

A job in fashion buying and range planning requires the following: the ability to recognize key trends; effective people skills, in orer to liaise with designers and suppliers; and good numeracy skills in order to calculate price and profit margins. The job involves analysing sales and product performance, reviewing competitors' ranges and negotiating with suppliers on product price and lead times. Flexibility is another important attribute as one day may involve being desk-bound and largely administrative whilst another will involve travelling to visit suppliers or to see new fashion ranges and trade fairs.

A TYPICAL CAREER PROGRESSION
ROUTE IN FASHION BUYING

BUYING DIRECTOR

BUYING MANAGER

SENIOR BUYER

JUNIOR BUYER

ASSISTANT OR TRAINEE BUYER

(Source: Goworek, 2007)

**1 NEW LOOK
SHOWROOMS**

UK retailer New Look closely
coordinates its design activities
with the merchandising and
buying teams and remains in
close contact with suppliers
to ensure product quality and
consistency are maintained
throughout production.

1

One quality that all good fashion buyers
tend to share is tacit knowledge: the ability
to instinctively know when something is right
or on trend. This knowledge cannot easily be
taught, although it may evolve over time: it
cannot be described as anything other than
flair and acumen for the product and a love
of fashion itself. It is an exciting job role but
not easy and at times it is highly pressurized,
requiring great stamina and the ability to
act quickly and with accuracy. Some buyers
may have been trained in a non-fashion
environment with a company that they may
not initially have considered working for.
Often the large international retailers will
have the best training programmes, which
are well worth considering.

Renowned buyers

Buyers with international reputation include
Marigay McKee at Harrods and Bridget
Cosgrave, formerly at Harvey Nichols and
now at Matches, London. There are many
others at large retailers whose skill set lies
in editing collections for their customers
and seeking out new and different brands
and designers. These talented individuals
can make designers famous and add
considerable gravitas to their success.
Joan Burstein, founder and owner of
Browns, London, has helped launch the
careers for many up-and-coming designers,
including John Galliano, Christopher Kane,
Mark Fast and Gareth Pugh.

The marketing mix: people

The role of the merchandiser

Every fashion retailer has a team of merchandisers, who bring the 'science' to match the 'art' provided by buyers and design teams. The merchandiser is the analytical and numerate figure of the key product development trio of designer, buyer and merchandiser.

The fashion merchandiser is involved in forecasting stock levels and analysing trends, allocating the stock and monitoring the sales of fashion products (and the colour, style and size in each style). Merchandisers will often talk about 'cover' of the stock levels, which refers to the number of weeks that stock is available for; there are many different ways of forecasting this cover and managing it in conjunction with suppliers. They will oversee deliveries and work very closely with manufacturers. These are the people who decide and agree big budgets, coordinate and assimilate clever promotions and maximize opportunities of the fashion ranges being bought and developed.

Merchandisers and buyers work together to agree stock levels and allocation. This involves allocating different ranges per store and which of these are to be volume or trial products. They will leave some level of fluidity within the budget allowing for in-season decisions for top-up orders or cancellations and room for the latest trend-led items. This is often referred to as 'open to buy' (OTB).

Fashion merchandising as a career

Fashion merchandising is a key function for the Arcadia Group, which owns Burton, Topshop and Miss Selfridge, amongst others. Its merchandisers work very closely with the buying and distribution teams. The first rung on the merchandising ladder at Arcadia is merchandise administrative assistant; there are about 100 such assistants in the group and they are mainly graduate recruits. Arcadia specifically looks for 'graduates who have studied analytical or business-type degrees, because the nature of the role is analysing sales figures and forecasting trends, so that we keep one step ahead to make sure profits are maximized.'

Many merchandisers have non-fashion backgrounds and may have a business or maths degree. The merchandiser must have the skills to deal with detailed pricing and flow charts and the ability to analyse statistical models. This means they can make fast and accurate decisions to ensure that the retailer can maximize the budget and therefore the profit margins for each fashion range.

'Merchandisers are responsible for ensuring that products appear in the right store at the right time and in the right quantities.'
www.prospects.ac.uk

1

CAREER PROGRESSION
IN FASHION MERCHANDISING

HEAD OF MERCHANDISING

(merchandisers often move into
supply chain roles such as supply chain
manager or director)

↑

MERCHANDISE MANAGER

↑

MERCHANDISER

↑

ASSISTANT MERCHANDISER

↑

TRAINEE MERCHANDISER

↑

ALLOCATOR

(Source: Goworek, 2007)

1 NEW LOOK
   SHOWROOMS

New Look operates a fast
fashion model, with emphasis
on in-house design, daily
orders and swift product
development, manufacture
and delivery.

Interview: Belinda Dickson

BELINDA DICKSON

Belinda Dickson OBE is a knitwear designer. Prior to launching her label, Belinda Robertson, Belinda worked for international fashion houses including Nina Ricci, Michael Kors and Dior. Whilst working in the Scottish Borders, Belinda developed an interest specifically in the cashmere knitwear industry and realized an ambition to give Scotland a 'good glamour label'. She recognized the potential of cashmere as a fashionable luxury item and, encouraged by a manufacturer, Belinda designed her first collection of cashmere couture. It was snapped up by the world-famous Burlington Arcade in London and Belinda Robertson launched in 1992.

Belinda has revolutionized knitwear design and production in a sector deep-rooted in tradition, and has successfully brought elegance, modernity and style to Scottish cashmere. The label Belinda set out to create almost 20 years ago has become a brand synonymous with pure luxury, exceptional quality and outstanding design: the finest cashmere in the world.

'We start with the shop first and then follow up with the website – communication with staff and customers is very important.'

Q How important is it for retailers to have a strategy?

A It is very important; it is a basic part of project planning in business and the fashion business is no different from any other. The retail strategy should cover everything: price, promotions, product development and so on.

It is vital that events at key times of the year are planned; this covers everything from the shop windows, websites and products. Sales teams need to work together with the website and planning stocks with the suppliers. Synchronization of these events is important but it is almost impossible to completely synchronize everything. We start with the shop first and then follow up with the website – communication with staff and customers is very important.

Q How often do you feel strategy and retail formats need to be reviewed?

A Strategy is about change: the fashion business is dominated by change; the environment changes and it is vital that we to respond to that. Levels of taxation import and export duty, the government, fuel prices, the weather, currency fluctuations; they can all make a difference to business and customers' spending habits.

The weather is notoriously difficult to predict in the UK and it really can make a difference, so we need to ensure that the products cover all eventualities. At some times of the year, in the knitwear business in particular, we sell more lightweight wraps and cardigans and it is vital that we need to manage the stock levels for this.

Interview: Belinda Dickson

Q The changes in fashion retail, in terms of speed to market, have impacted on designers and much of the high street. Do you agree?

A Buyers increasingly want to buy short and allow for buying more during the season so we must create flexibility by having short lead times. They want to leave the decision-making later and keep as much budget open to buy as possible.

A lot can change during the season – it's dependent on sales performance – so there needs to be two large stock deliveries in season with two smaller ones mid-season and continual top-ups as well.

Companies at mass-market level, such as Zara and Primark, have really tackled this initiative and are leading the market with their supply chains. Manufacturers that can turn stock around quickly and in the correct quantities with flexible lead times will win orders from fashion brands and retailers.

Q How has online shopping affected and changed the way in which fashion retailers operate?

A It is an absolutely essential tool that fashion retailers need as a part of the package of services available to customers. Customers often do their research and source products online, especially if visiting a city or country that is new to them; they will find out what is available in the shops before they arrive.

'Fashion retailing is about huge attention to detail. Buying the product well is key to success but by far the most difficult thing is keeping the stock moving and planning stock levels and maintaining your cash flow. Sometimes you have to plan for worst-case scenarios.'

Q Do you see changes in sourcing policy and manufacturing as continuing?

A Absolutely and it's very challenging. Now many manufacturers want payments up front, ahead of production – it ties up your cash flow with no guarantee of stock on time. Exchange rate fluctuation is another problem at times.

Quality is another challenge: in fact, you need to put measures in place for this; having a third party to negotiate and manage quality of the supply chain is a necessity now.

Shipping lead times can take two months by sea from China – you have to weigh up the cost versus time of air or sea shipments. In fact always add room for error here: a good risk management procedure, as part of strategy, is needed with manufacturing.

Many fashion retailers now use samples to photograph fashion products on models for the websites and when the orders come in then the orders are consolidated and placed. However, this means customers may have to wait after placing an order.

Interview: Belinda Dickson

Q How important is the product development process to your business and its design strategy and adapting your designs to the market?

A This really depends upon the brand and the customers' requirements. If you are involved in fast fashion you would need to be very aggressive about changes in fashion products. A luxury or niche brand, which tends to have a very loyal customer, sells more classic fashion products that they tend to be known for. However, even the classics need a twist! A clever strategy is required, as the customer will expect replacement products to be 'tweaked' to suit fashion; there may often be a technical reason for change, such as to improve fit and shape or other fabric and yarn improvements to the products.

Q How you see the future of fashion in terms of retail strategy?

A The future is so hard to predict; for example we could not have envisaged the impact of online shopping and retailing – it was an unknown. But I can see more technological change, in effect creating 'bespoke' products, like the interactive changing rooms that photograph and measure customers in order to create an individual fit. Individuality in the mass market is more relevant to some customers.

The super brands have taken over the market and many high streets and shopping malls look and feel the same; it is a trend from the USA that has spread but in a smaller country, such as the UK, it seems more concentrated. More niche, bespoke retailers with personal service may regain popularity, as will better quality products – the throwaway society in which we live has taken over in the western world. We have too many clothes! Less is more.

Q What is a typical day or week in the season like for you?

A My typical day starts very early. It is vital to have that time to plan: organize my priorities and check emails before the phone starts ringing so that I do not waste time later in the day. I check email three times a day on average. If you prepare each day and have a plan for each week, with a priority list that may change, it's a good way to start.

If each day is managed and planned, then as other issues crop up they can be dealt with effectively. On average, my planning time over a season looks a bit like this: planning and strategic direction 20–25%; R&D product development time 15–20%; sales and distribution 40%; general administration is around 15%.

Planning is my priority – you can easily have great products and sell them badly. Marketing is crucial to the success of the strategic planning process in fashion retailing. It may sound like a cliché but the four Ps of price, place, position and promotion are vital to the strategic planning process in the fashion business.

'Each season you go back to the start of the process, unlike any other business, and you are only as good as the last season. Build on your successes if you can and ensure that the execution of everything you do is the absolute best in order to succeed.'

Case study: Topshop

Topshop is a part of the Arcadia Group owned by the British entrepreneur and retailer Sir Philip Green. It originally began trading as a concession within Peter Robinson, London, in 1964 and became independent in 1974. The Arcadia Group is the UK's largest privately owned clothing retailer with more than 2,500 outlets. It owns seven of the UK high street's best-known fashion brands, each with its own distinctive identity and market segment: Burton; Dorothy Perkins; Evans; Miss Selfridge; Topman; Topshop and Wallis.

Arcadia has increased online presence. The Arcadia e-commerce operation is significant and rapidly expanding as a part of its multi-channel service offer. Arcadia brands also operate in over 30 countries across Europe, the Far East and the Middle East via 420 international franchise stores.

Creating a competitive advantage

Topshop is renowned for its cutting-edge, high fashion looks, which include a mixture of own brands and designer ranges. It has been described as 'fashion Disney' thanks to its exciting and continually changing store environment. Added to this mix are catwalk looks that are delivered swiftly to stores via short lead times from key manufacturing bases. Topshop targets a young customer with fashionable tastes; it uses an exciting store retail format and image as part of its competitive advantage to attract customers.

The retailer is continually evolving its position and expanding internationally. It is this retail strategy that has enabled Topshop to retain its position as market leader; it maximizes its competitive advantage on the UK high street and has the ability to capitalize on a fast-growing worldwide reputation.

Topshop.com features over 300 new products each week, offering additional editorial features such as fashion and styling advice. It also offers a designer collection, Topshop Unique, which shows at London Fashion Week and is available to customers via the website.

Designer collaborations

Topshop was one of the first high street retailers to offer designer collaborations and celebrity ranges. The Kate Moss collaboration, for example, has been hugely successful. Other capsule collections by up-and-coming designers include Christopher Kane, Jonathan Saunders, Preen and Dexter Wong. There are also collaborations with more established names, such as a Topman menswear range by the legendary rock 'n' roll tailor Antony Price, who dressed Bryan Ferry, David Bowie and Duran Duran in the 1980s.

Topshop runs a young designers programme called NewGen, which offers London Fashion Week sponsorship. Designers who are selected receive around £100,000 to produce their collections and a catwalk show. Topshop then uses this to its competitive advantage by selling versions or part of these collections in stores; this is how Christopher Kane became involved with the retailer.

'[We] recently expanded the online offer to shoppers around the world with 12 new shipping destinations… this expansion means our customers can get full access to iconic British style straight to the door from over 30 countries… customers can also access it via the Topshop, Facebook and Twitter pages.'
Topshop

TOPSHOP ON THE RUNWAY

In 2005, Topshop's Unique collection became the first high-street range to be shown on the catwalk as part of the official schedule of London Fashion Week.

Case study: Topshop

International expansion

In 2009 Topshop continued its international retail format expansion by opening a $20 million New York store, designed by UK firm Dalziel and Pow. Following this initial success, Topshop then swiftly opened a second New York store six months later. The first New York store features floor-to-ceiling display windows on every level for 'an army of mannequins'; it features original beams, columns, reclaimed timber floors and old brick with futuristic lighting and a DJ booth suspended over the heads of shoppers. The New York stores are the first of a roll-out plan of stores across the USA: shops are planned for Miami, Los Angeles, Las Vegas and Boston. Further European expansion is also now likely.

Green has cited his intentions to work with the legendary Diane von Furstenberg, president of the CFDA (Council of Fashion Designers of America) and Anna Wintour, editor-in-chief of American *Vogue*, with a view to showcasing young American designers; an initiative that Wintour has undertaken with other retailers such as Gap.

Marketing mix: position

The boutique atmosphere of the stores and the funky, irreverent British fashion is an eclectic combination; it combines the success factors for fashion retail, addressing the key components in the marketing mix: product price, position and place. One of Topshop's strengths is its Britishness; a factor it played up in the US stores, using British decorative icons such as bicycles, pigeons and Union Jack flags.

All of this has only emphasized its competitive edge and no doubt given the surrounding stores (such as Anthropologie, Victoria Secret, Barneys and Diesel, all of whom have a reputation for great visual merchandising and original mixtures of brands and store formats) a shock to the system.

'Topshop has realized that one of the most important determinants of success is retail store image.'
Amirani & Gates cited by Newman & Patel, 2004

GLOBAL EXPANSION

In 2011, Arcadia boss Sir Philip Green announced plans to double Topshop's profits through overseas expansion, most notably with a string of 100%-owned stores across the United States.

Case study: Topshop

'It's not a question of winding down in the UK. We want to do flagship stores here but overseas we haven't even scratched the surface. There's a lot to do. Topshop exports well because it has an identity and a point of view.'
Sir Philip Green

Key to success

This is successful fashion retailing at its best: new locations, exciting products at affordable prices and innovative store environments to create a distinctive retail experience for customers. Topshop plays on its British heritage whilst providing something unique for its international market.

In addition, Topshop offers continually improving service levels and offers, such as online sales and the continuation of its 10% student discount offer in the USA. All of this has helped Topshop tap into the potential of a great new market via a clever positioning strategy. It will be interesting to see how far it intends to pursue an international strategy and expand its market in direct competition with other large-scale fashion retailers in the same market sector, such as Zara and H&M. Topshop seems unstoppable in its attempt to maintain and grow market position and to become a truly international fashion brand and retailer.

RETAIL STRATEGY

Topshop has a unique, irreverent brand image. It capitalizes on the fast-moving fashion cycle: as new trends emerge, within weeks they can be found in Topshop stores.

Chapter 3 summary

This chapter has examined the concept of retail strategy and
the ways in which a fashion business addresses the increasingly
competitive marketplace. We have seen that it is important to
identify and analyse the competition and to understand the business's
strengths and weaknesses alongside those of the competition.
In addition, we discussed the components for strategic analysis:
market position, place, price and people. A regular review of the
strength and viability of fashion products and the provision of
customer service is essential for a successful retail strategy.

Questions and discussion points

We have examined the ways in which fashion
businesses develop retail strategy; consider the
following questions in connection with this and your
understanding of chapter three:

1. Identify the different types of fashion retailers in your
   local shopping area. What are the key differences that
   you see between the retail formats?

2. Identify some retailers' own brands or labels and
   analyse them: how similar are they compared with
   the well-known brands available?

3. How effective are department stores at presenting
   new designers' ranges and introducing new
   innovative product offers?

4. What sort of promotions or sales do you see at the
   moment in your nearest shopping outlet or city?
   How effective are they?

5. How do these sales or promotions differ by retailer?
   What sort of price ranges can you identify and what
   are the levels of discount?

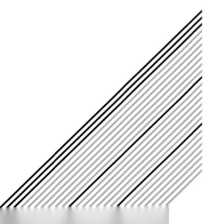

Exercises

The following exercises are designed to make you think like a buyer or merchandiser. They are known in the fashion industry as comparative shop exercises and are regularly conducted as part of competitive analysis.

1. Visit two different retailers in two different types of market sector. Analyse the competition to these retailers: who are they competing with and why?

2. Visit the websites of retailers that are only online and those that are multi-channel retailers. What differences, if any, do you see?

3. Price: what are the key differences of products that you see online and in stores in different price categories? Are there differences in relation to fabric, design, colour, packaging or designer labels?

4. In your opinion, and based on your research, put a list together of the top ten products you have found based on good price, quality and fashionability.

5. Try to develop a new strategy for a company or brand that you consider to be 'tired' or in need of a makeover. What would you like to do differently?

4

THE SUPPLY CHAIN

In this chapter we examine supply chain management (SCM) and consider why it is important to the fashion business and merchandising. If fashion retailers and businesses get it right, SCM has massive potential rewards. There is a fast-growing belief amongst fashion retailers that all people involved in the supply chain – from designers, buyers and merchandisers to suppliers and production managers – should have in-depth working knowledge of all the functions. It is vital to understand that SCM begins with the customer and that it does not end with them.

1 BENETTON FACTORY

Benetton redesigned its production system in 2005, evolving from an organization based on divisions (such as wool and cotton) to a structure based on service units (such as planning and quality control). The new system enabled a more efficient, flexible and integrated supply chain.

The textile industry

It is useful to understand industrialization, within the context of the textiles industry, in order to examine supply chain management in more detail.

According to Bell (1963), the industrialization of countries can be divided into three categories:

- × Pre-industrial
- × Industrial
- × Post-industrial

A key characteristic of a post-industrial society is a growth in the service sector of activity and employment. This includes fashion retailing, which is a significant part of the service sector.

The UK, the USA and Canada, Australia, Japan and most countries in the EU have evolved from being industrial to post-industrial economies. The figures in the EU, for example, show that the service sector has risen from 35–45% in 1960 to 60–75% today. Pre-industrial economies include countries where there are still large cottage industries: most of Africa, for example, and the Indian sub-continent. China is a notable example of a country that has moved to the industrial phase.

Textiles were a major part of the 'first' industrial revolution, centred in Lancashire in the UK. Manchester, in the UK, was known as the 'Cottonopolis'; it has been described as the first global industrial city. The industrial revolution of the textile industry rapidly spread to northern Europe in the late 18th century and then to the USA. We are currently witnessing a new industrial revolution in China and SE Asia, which has developed in a much shorter period of time.

1 POST-INDUSTRIAL SCM

Supply chain management in post-industrial countries represents a paradigm shift in manufacturing: from local to global sourcing.

'*The world's five major apparel markets (US, EU, China, India and Japan) will more than double in the next decade.*'
Hale & Wills, 2002

1

Supply chain management

There are several key concepts in SCM that have emerged over the last 20 years. These include so-called fast fashion or quick response models. Collaborative relationships in SCM, where relevant in the chain, are crucial to global supply chain success. Ethical issues have emerged as a result of international sourcing, creating a real need for these relationships to be based upon trust and shared values of the supplier and brand.

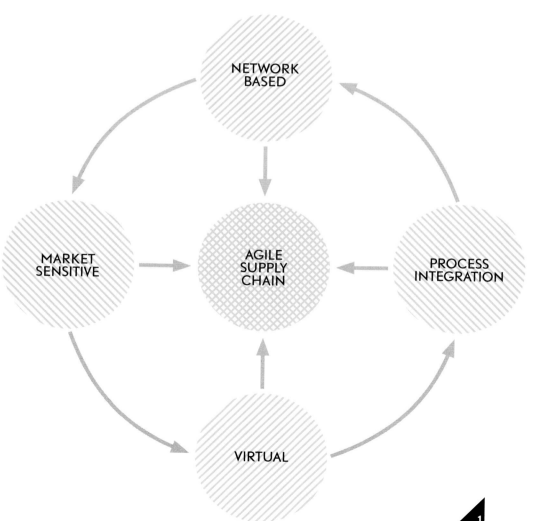

1

The Four Rs

Martin Christopher developed a theory known as the Four Rs, which works in a similar way to the marketing mix: reliability; resilience; responsiveness and relationships. These factors should be considered by brands and retailers when developing or changing the supply chain strategy and, indeed, managing it.

Fast fashion models of supply

Quick response (QR) manufacturing techniques have accelerated the impact for more effective supply chain management. QR has been defined as 'a search for a reduction in lead times' (Christopher, 2000) and has helped to establish relationships in supply chains.

Although fashion retailer Zara is credited with introducing fast fashion to the mass market, it did in fact grow out of QR techniques developed some years before. Described as the evolution of **lean and agile** supply chains, QR manufacturing developed in the USA, with retailers and manufacturers who had to respond to a loss in market share to suppliers from the Far East in the 1980s. The brand probably most well known for pioneering the QR model in clothing is The Limited, a part of MAST industries, which maximized manufacturing to produce ranges for its Express and Limited brands. This model developed into what we now refer to as fast fashion.

Lean and agile

Naylor et al (1999) provide a useful definition of the two paradigms as follows: 'Agility means using market knowledge and a virtual corporation to exploit profitable opportunities in a volatile marketplace... Leanness means developing a value stream to eliminate all waste including time, and to enable a level schedule.'

1 QUICK RESPONSE
   MODEL OF SUPPLY

Quick response (QR) is a market-driven business strategy focused on providing shorter lead times. QR enables orders to be placed closer to the start of the selling season and, typically for fashion products, QR lowers lead time by one to four months (Skinner, 1992).

Supply chain management

SCM strategy

The SCM strategy of a fashion business should reflect the company and its business strategy. An effective supply chain strategy should be market-driven and customer focused, with strong links between the buying and product development processes. Good critical path management is absolutely crucial to the success of SCM strategy; it closely monitors the progress of each step from product development to production.

SCM strategy is driven by globalization and fast-fashion retail models. Businesses should focus on their core competencies – in other words, they must consider what they are good at.

Some of the key points for a fashion business supply chain to review include:
× Cost
× Speed to market
× Reliability
× Flexibility
× Responsiveness (ability to react to sales)

These points can all contribute to making a business/retailer unique or special, often referred to as a unique selling point (**USP**).

Relationships in SCM

Relationships in SCM are vital to success: buyers, merchandisers and designers alike need to understand the implications of supply chain decisions and decide together where it is appropriate to add value and where they need to reduce cost. An effective supply chain creates value for the customer at an acceptable cost, margin and selling price.

There are many types of suppliers and manufacturers available to fashion retailers and they can provide different levels of service.

USP

Prahalad and Hamel (1994), define USP as 'a bundle of skills and technology that enables a business to provide a benefit to customers.'

Supplier types

It is important to consider what is required and to build good relationships in supply chains where they are most needed. There are three main supplier types:

× Direct supply. The retailer has total control of the process, which requires a high level of input; this is often referred to as 'buying FOB' (the ex-factory price = freight on board). The retailer arranges own transport and duty and sends all the information to the manufacturer.

× Agent. This is a sales and design team that acts as a go-between, arranging visits, managing orders, fielding calls and negotiations. Agents Li and Fung, based in Hong Kong, are known as global 'super sourcers' and they work with hundreds of factories and retailers in south-east Asia.

× Full-service vendor (FSV). This is usually a world-class, large-scale manufacturer, which can offer benefits for retailers. The FSV will organize transportation, duty and all exportation, providing good service levels from first samples to final-fit approval.

When making decisions about which suppliers to work with, the following must be considered: lead times, communication and costs involved to the retailer as well as reliability, ability and flexibility. Different products require different types of supplier; it is not a case of 'one size fits all'.

The Japanese were at the forefront of innovation in supply chain relationships in the automobile industry and they were one of the first to invest in the chain of manufacturing. This led to semi-vertical relationships via collaboration and coordination in the chain and also investment in people. This type of collaboration then spread to the clothing industry with techniques such as 'just in time' (JIT): 'a common supply chain concept in the apparel industry; it is the delivery of finished goods without carrying excess stock but in time to meet the market demand' (Bruce, 2004).

'Accompanying this recognition of the importance of the process has been a fundamental shift in the focus of the business towards the marketplace and away from the more inwardly oriented production and sales mentality that previously dominated most industries.'
Christopher, 1988

Global sourcing

Supply chain management represents a paradigm shift in the manufacturing of goods and what this means generally is a shift away from local to global sourcing. Globalization has had both positive and negative effects on manufacturing and purchasing behaviour alike.

Drivers for change

There are a number of drivers of SCM and global sourcing trends. These are:

1. The combination of reduced labour costs and a readily available, flexible workforce enable shorter critical path or lead times – essential for fast fashion.

2. Advances in technology: the increased speed of the Internet and the evolution of trend forecasting websites have provided fashion retailers with fast access to catwalk trends. Technological change has made replication of products easier and faster.

3. The elimination of quotas and the end of the **Multi Fibre Arrangement** (MFA) has created a truly global industry. In the EU and USA there is now easy access to Asian markets for the quick production of cheap clothing.

4. Government incentives: the UK government, for example, created incentives for fashion retailers to produce goods in poorer countries such as Bangladesh, Sri Lanka and Mauritius.

5. It is important to note that sourcing is a moving target and the recession has driven customer desire for lower-priced fashion even further. By way of illustration, sales at UK discount fashion retailer Primark rose by around 18–20% between 2009 and 2010.

Multi Fibre Arrangement

The Multi Fibre Arrangement (MFA) was established in 1974 to govern world trade in textiles and garments. Under the MFA, Canada, the USA and the EU imposed quotas on the amount of apparel and textiles that could be imported from 73 developing countries, mostly in Asia. The quotas were phased out over a ten-year period and finally eliminated on 1 January 2005.

1 EFFECTS OF
   GLOBALIZATION

Garment factory in Vinales, Cuba. Production and manufacturing are being relocated to countries that have cheap, readily available labour. Employment options in Cuba are slim and people are willing to work long hours for modest pay.

1

Effects of globalization

Cheaper imports and greater efficiency has opened up new markets, created high demand and new opportunities. There has also been a shift in production to higher value consumer goods such as cashmere and leather. It has created employment growth in some parts of the world where manufacturing has become centralized. Production and manufacturing has been relocated to low-cost countries with cheap, flexible labour. There are now more working women and there is a greater need for increased flexibility in the workplace.

However, the changing employment structure within post-industrialized countries has led to broad-scale polarization of income distribution, such as unemployment coupled with an ageing population. In the EU and USA there has been an increase of one-person households. All of these issues create opportunities and threats for fashion retailers and there has been a change in the broad-scale structure of customer consumption.

The key to success is for retailers and designers to try to recognize and anticipate consumer change. Key differences and change in customer attitudes are crucial to retailers when devising product ranges and retail store formats and in redeveloping supply chains. It is only certain that change will occur even more rapidly in the future as globalization continues; its impact is felt most acutely in supply chains.

Global sourcing

Geographical areas of expertise

China

This region was originally famous for silk and cashmere, its tailoring skills and hand-embellished products.

The ending of the MFA (see page 110) has opened up this market and therefore its enormous and skilled labour force. China is the world's fastest growing world economy and the government has made major investments in its technology, road and rail infrastructure. China is often referred to as the 'factory of the world'.

India

India has the second fastest growing world economy, with large-scale textile production, especially cotton and silk fibres. It specializes in colour, woven, printed cloth and denim. There is a widely available labour force that largely speaks and understands English. The Indian government has invested in its manufacturing industry to enable development.

Sri Lanka

Sri Lanka is now an established world class manufacturer of fashion clothing, via joint ventures and also wholly owned Sri Lankan companies. It has a well-established joint apparel association forum, with businesses intending to advance from manufacturing to becoming full service vendors.

Turkey

Turkey's close proximity to Europe and wide availability of cotton jersey fabrics and denim makes it a good local manufacturing option for European brands. Transport links are well established and there is a solid understanding of the fashion industry with relatively sophisticated manufacturing. Well known for products such as nightwear and swimwear, it is often referred to as a fast fashion hub.

Mexico and Central America

Manufacturers here are vulnerable to cheaper overseas imports and more expensive than those in Asia but are useful and relevant to USA brands and retailers who may have preferential duty and import rates (see <www.clothesource.com>).

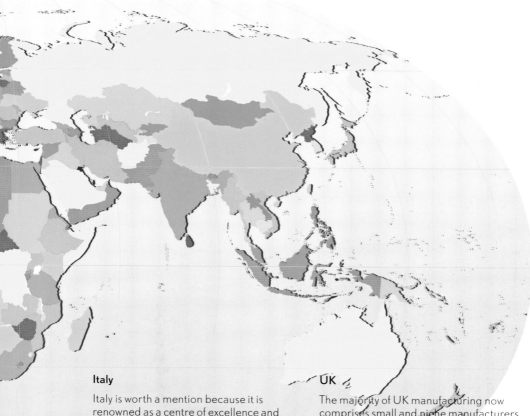

Italy

Italy is worth a mention because it is renowned as a centre of excellence and craftsmanship particularly in textiles, silk and leather. Traditionally centred in and around Prato and Como in northern Italy, the industry is now in decline and only the very exclusive brands can afford to manufacture here. The Italian government has protected the remaining industry to support the designers. However, in order to survive, many Italian companies have employed migrant workers or else relocated overseas.

UK

The majority of UK manufacturing now comprises small and niche manufacturers, which tend to be specialist and expensive. Some examples include knitwear in Hawick, Scotland and John Smedley, which still produces its specialist knitwear in Derbyshire, England. (Details of other UK manufacturers can be found at <www.ukft.com>.)

USA

As with Italy and the UK, garment manufacturing is in decline, due to technological advances and imports of apparel and textiles. Manufacturing has become highly automated and must be labour-efficient to compete effectively with foreign manufacturers. Nearly half of garment manufacture is based in three states: California, North Carolina and Georgia.

Risk management

Risk management in the supply chain has become a big issue. All risks must be considered and identified by those involved in the supply chain from product development through to manufacturing and distribution, especially in the context of global sourcing. All business involves some degree of risk and the fashion business is no different from any other in this respect, although it should be noted that demand for products in the fashion industry is more unpredictable than in other industries: sales can easily be higher or lower than predicted.

The outsourcing and sub-contracting of manufacturing means retailers can easily lose visibility of the production of goods and raw materials. Retailers are usually located thousands of miles away from their manufacturers or suppliers, which is one of the most difficult areas for risk management. Goods are at risk of being damaged or stolen in transit. Additionally, there may be unforeseen delays in delivery due to weather conditions and natural disasters – this can be anything from flooding or snow to severe problems such as earthquakes. Another issue with global sourcing is changes in export or import tariffs and fuel costs and fluctuations in currency rates – all of which affect the cost price of a garment. To negate the impact of these risks it makes sense for retailers to have a spread of different suppliers in different regions as well as the appropriate skill set.

At the product development end of the process it is easy to miss deadlines for production; designs may be misinterpreted by manufacturers or replicated by other retailers who are using the same supplier. Staff turnover can also present risks, particularly within buying, merchandising and design teams. Employees will often move around, sometimes to the competition, and may take information with them: this is difficult to prevent but can be managed.

It is essential for retailers to undertake careful risk assessment and implement a robust risk management process in SCM. If fashion retailers work with the correct partners and build good relationships in SCM, then they are likely to be more reliable and flexible and implementation of any agreements or process will be much simpler to adhere to. In addition, it is important for a business to review its **key performance indicators**, which can be used each season to review the effectiveness, reliability, quality, responsiveness and flexibility of partners in the supply chain.

Key performance indicators

A business will often create measures to monitor its performance and that of its suppliers. These measures are known as key performance indicators (KPIs).

1 RISK MANAGEMENT IN
THE SUPPLY CHAIN

A successful risk management
strategy involves the
assessment and evaluation
of potential risks and
management measures,
from product development
through to manufacturing
and distribution.

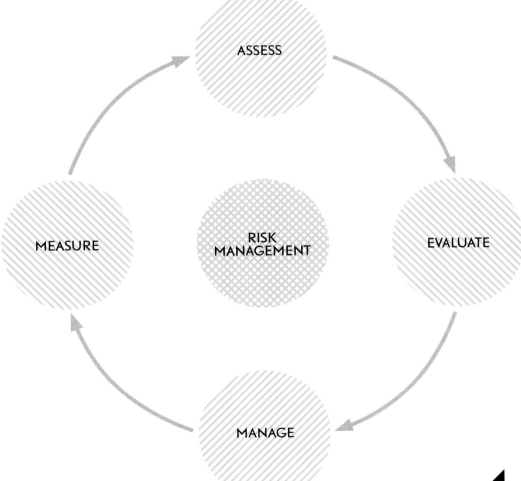

1

Logistics and outsourcing in the supply chain

To introduce the subject of logistics, which is a vital part of outsourcing in the chain, we must first understand that all organizations and businesses have to move materials: fashion moves all the time. Manufacturers build factories that collect raw materials from suppliers and deliver finished goods. Logistics is the management of the movement of materials between suppliers and customers and the logistics provider is responsible for bringing all the parts together; they are the link in the supply chain.

There are various reasons why retailers and fashion businesses have invested in logistics: these include rising costs, competition and internationalization. There are further opportunities to reduce costs by creating efficient transport and distribution systems. In marketing terms, an effective logistics strategy will enable a retailer to deliver promises to its customers: in other words, goods on time.

Reducing cost

In the supply chain products should flow as if passing through a pipeline. Stock should be continually moving to keep costs down: in production, in transit, in a container or on a ship, then into a distribution centre and out to stores. Stock that stands still does not add value, only cost.

Logistics has been described as the 'last cost-saving frontier' in a business, creating productivity and value. SCM is now regarded as a key element in customer service and logistics is an important basis for differentiation. The shift to international sourcing and distribution has created further complexity of logistical operations and many retailers and fashion companies will outsource this highly specialized part of the supply chain to companies such as DHL/EXEL, Allport and Amtrak. These specialists handle all of the transportation and collection of goods and organize documentation ready for export.

1

'Formalized supply chain management is increasingly being recognized as a critical determinant of competitive advantage.'
Christopher, 1997

2

To illustrate the importance of good logistics and an efficient supply chain, let us compare retailers Marks & Spencer and Zara. Marks & Spencer stayed with British manufacturers long after its competition moved products overseas with a quality, service and price balance difference. It lost market share as a result and had to change supply chain direction in order to regain its competitiveness. Zara, on the other hand, became leaders in implementing a quick-response supply chain model, rapidly growing into an international fashion brand.

The main activities of a logistics provider include:

× The procurement or purchasing of raw materials
× Inward-bound transport (such as fabric)
× The receipt of goods
× Warehousing or storage of goods at port, with the manufacturer or in a distribution centre (DC)
× Stock control
× Order picking
× Material handling
× Outward transport (to the port)
× Physical distribution of stock via distribution centres
× Recycling and returns (reverse logistics)
× Location of stock in the chain
× Communication with manufacturers and the retailers

1+2 INDITEX LOGISTICS

The Inditex Group owns Zara, amongst other brands. Its workshop network enables a high degree of production flexibility with a lead-in time of just three weeks. Designs may be altered and new versions created throughout the season.

Logistics and outsourcing in the supply chain

CPFR models

Quick response in logistics and SCM ensures product innovation in the market: the logistics supplier can deliver the vision of designers and buyers, reduce and minimize disturbances in the chain and coordinate and consolidate goods, which is especially important when launching new products and ranges. Data collection and the appropriate and relevant technology must be in place for this to work properly. One such example is a Collaborative Planning Forecasting and Replenishment (CPFR) model of supply. CPFR is 'a business practice which reduces inventory costs whilst improving product availability across the chain. Trading partners share forecast and results data over the Internet. CPFR data analyses data and alerts planners and merchandisers at each company to exceptional situations that may affect delivery or sales performance' (Hines, 2005). Trading partners collaborate to resolve these exceptions in the chain in order to maintain stock and availability. CPFR models have been replicated and adapted for use by many large, international fashion retailers in order to make suppliers responsible for stock management. Good stock management is crucial to success in the fashion industry.

Future of technology

Some large, international retailers are investing in new technological models of supply, including retail exchanges and e-tail logistics, such as the global net exchange (GNX) and the worldwide retail exchange (WWRE) developed by Walmart.

Technology helps fashion retailers with sales information that can be transferred and acted upon quickly. These include the following: EDI (electronic data information) packages for sharing data between supply chain partners; EPOS – electronic point-of-sale data collection from stores; and SBO, which is sales-based ordering technology (orders placed to replenish sold stock).

Other technology used in SCM includes electronic tagging radio frequency identification tags. Walmart piloted a study in the USA and UK fashion retailer Marks & Spencer has trialled its use on high-value items such as suits and leather jackets. The tags can be used to achieve good visibility in the chain; retailers such as Benetton, Gap and Esprit use the tags to track stock movement in the supply chain. They can be used during transportation and warehousing so logistics teams can identify stock, size and colour without unpacking boxes and by scanning stock that is packaged.

It cannot be emphasized enough that good relationships and outsourcing are fundamental to the future success of SCM in the fashion business and improvements in technology may be used to enhance these relationships. The focus is on fashion retailers in the future to provide better value and to create greater responsiveness via partnerships.

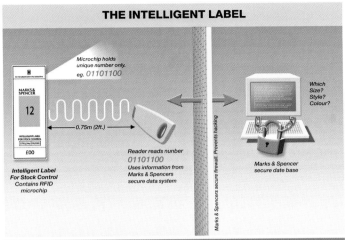

THE INTELLIGENT LABEL

Microchip holds unique number only. eg. *01101100*

MARKS & SPENCER

12

INTELLIGENT LABEL FOR STOCK CONTROL
STYLE No: 2XXXXX

£00

Intelligent Label For Stock Control Contains RFID microchip

0.75m (2ft.)

Reader reads nunber *01101100* Uses information from Marks & Spencers secure data system

Marks & Spencers secure firewall. Prevents hacking

Which Size? Style? Colour?

Marks & Spencer secure date base

HOW THE INTELLIGENT LABEL IS USED FOR STOCK CONTROL

1 Microchip in Label holds a unique number

2 Final Printer adds UPC barcode and reads chip number

3 Intelligent Labels sent to factory for attachment to garments

UPC and chip number sent back to UK

4 Finished garments despatched to UK Distribution Centre

Accurate stock date converted to UPC's and sent to stock database

Store order sent to DC

Secure stock database updated

M&S Secure RFID Platform

Scanned Chip Numbers

5 Stored in D.C.

6 Customer assistant scans stock on display

10 Customer removes label after purchase

9 Every size & style available for customer

8 Missing sizes and styles sent to store

7 D.C. team pick new stock based on accurate date

YOUR M&S

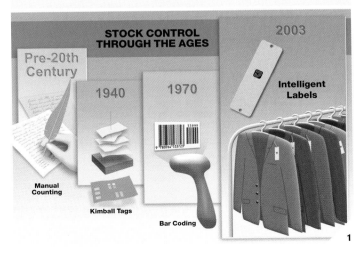

STOCK CONTROL THROUGH THE AGES

Pre-20th Century

1940

1970

2003

Intelligent Labels

Manual Counting

Kimball Tags

Bar Coding

9 780764 533729

1 ELECTRONIC TAGGING

UK retailer Marks & Spencer has trialled the use of electronic tagging radio frequency identification tags on high-value items such as suits and leather jackets.

1

Ethics in the supply chain

1

Fashion supply chains are predominantly driven by fast clothing and disposability; they rely on the ability of manufacturers to switch production on and off and the ability of the brand to relocate for speed to market and margin pressures. However, public pressure from campaigners and NGOs (non-government organizations) has created a major force for change. Retailers are being forced to pay closer attention to the ways in which their goods are produced: bad publicity surrounding ethics is not good for business.

Fashion retailers and manufacturers must consider their global impact as they continue to develop products overseas and expand in new markets (both in terms of selling and manufacturing). The ethics of local and global supply, associated labour issues and their impact upon local communities are increasingly important.

1 ORGANIC COTTON
  FARMING

Farmer Nouhoum Bamba at the Kolanjeba Organic Cotton Farm in Mali. Ethical designer and campaigner Katharine Hamnett was invited by Oxfam to visit Mali in 2003 to highlight the plight of the cotton farmers due to western cotton subsidies.

The development of good relationships between retailers and apparel brands, manufacturers and outsourcing is crucial for the future success of SCM. All parties need to work together to formulate the best way of working. This is not an easy dynamic at times when the pressure to reduce cost and optimize speed is the main criteria in a competitive fashion retail environment. However, in today's environmentally concerned society it is simply unacceptable to exploit those, such as factory workers in developing countries, who have less of a voice.

The demand for ethical goods

The views of consumers can influence and pressurize retailers and their suppliers. There is increased market demand for fair trade and organic products and traceability of raw materials. According to a Mintel report (2009), the UK's ethical fashion industry is currently worth approximately £175 million. It states, 'The widening availability of ethical fashion is central to this growth. Real choice in styling and quality and truly fashionable design has been vital in the market's development.' According to the Co-operative (2008), ethical fashion in the UK is growing faster than almost any other ethical sector, at 71% per year.

However, consumers may often say one thing and do another, especially when they want to buy fashion items at a good price. The style and cost of the garment is often the decision-making factor, not its ethical credentials. In times of economic uncertainty, consumer demand for cheap clothing remains high and the expectations are for immediacy or instant gratification in fashion retail purchasing behaviour. It remains that one of the most important issues for retailers is to provide customers with the right products at a realistic cost.

Ethical issues

- × Fair trade
- × Child labour
- × Workers' rights and pay
- × Working conditions
- × Carbon footprint
- × Organic textiles
- × Air miles of clothing
- × Animal welfare
- × Textile technology: recycled and biodegradable fibres
- × Global warming
- × Supplier relationships

'Failure to react quickly to fashion demand can result in missing significant sales and/or demand may have abated by the time the product reaches the store resulting in less time to make profit and higher risk of obsolescence.'
Christopher, 2004

Ethics in the supply chain

Corporate Social Responsibility (CSR)

CSR and business ethics are often used interchangeably but are quite different. CSR is related to the social contract between a business and the society in which it operates. It sets out the intentions of the business to behave and operate responsibly with its sourcing and supply chain and in its overall business strategy. Most large businesses, such as Marks & Spencer, Monsoon, H&M and Gap, will have a CSR policy within their corporate and marketing strategy and this will generally be widely promoted. CSR policy can usually be found on a company's website, illustrating how that brand or retailer implements it within its business. Businesses are increasingly using CSR as part of their key performance measures and this can have an impact on the bottom line: profit.

Cause-related marketing (CRM) is an offshoot of CSR. The idea is that aligning companies with certain causes will create social capital in the business. A great example of this is the RED campaign, which helps those with Aids in Africa, in which GAP, American Express and Motorola are involved, amongst others.

Many fashion retailers use ethical initiatives and turn them into valuable marketing and corporate strategy, which may then be used to gain competitive advantage. It is clear that some fashion brands do far more than others to enhance the visibility and ethical nature of their supply chains. However, whilst responsible retailers may take an ethical stance in their marketing campaigns, this, alongside a demand for fast fashion can present challenges: the two do not sit comfortably together.

1   BENETTON COLORS

COLORS magazine is published by the Benetton group. It was established in 1991 with the premise that 'diversity is positive but that all cultures have equal value'. It is a good example of a brand using CRM to competitive advantage.

'Consumers may hold ethical companies in high regard but do not necessarily buy their products because of it... such consumers will only buy ethically if it does not detract from the value and brand and involves no inconvenience.'
Carrigan and Hall, 2001

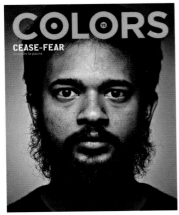

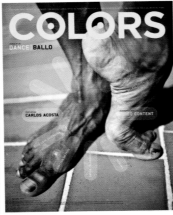

Ethics in the supply chain

The role of NGOs

NGOs are defined by the World Bank as 'private organizations that pursue activities to relieve suffering, promote the interests of the poor, protect the environment, provide basic social services, or undertake community development.'

Labour issues in the garment industry are well documented and it is the role of the NGOs to work with fashion retailers to establish and improve their labour policies and to help protect workers' rights. Examples include Oxfam, which works in the interest of creating rights for workers and conditions overseas. The International Labour Organization (ILO), a UN agency established in 1919, is jointly governed by government, employer and worker representatives. Its mission is to raise global awareness and understanding of labour issues, to eliminate forced and child labour. Labour Behind the Label is a network of organizations that support workers worldwide, helping them to 'improve their working conditions, through awareness raising, information provision and encouraging international solidarity between workers and consumers.' In addition to working in the industry, Labour Behind the Label works with colleges and fashion students to promote knowledge and understanding of the issues that may confront buyers, merchandisers, designers and anyone else involved in sourcing.

The ETI

Fashion retailers' policies vary wildly but should all be based on the guidelines set out by the World Trade Organization (WTO). A member organization called the Ethical Trading Initiative (ETI) is a good example of an NGO that is influencing and helping shape retail policy. The initiative, launched in the UK in 1997, bases its policies on WTO guidelines. It is relevant to note here that there is little, if any, legislation in place to force retailers and manufacturers to join an organization such as the ETI and to adhere to guidelines. But by becoming a member, a company is making a commitment to tackle issues within its supply chains. The ETI's member companies are expected to report annually on their efforts and results and to show improvement in their ethical trade performance.

'Until very recently, a fashion buyer or buying team would rarely engage directly with suppliers – neither fabric manufacturers nor fibre – but barriers are coming down. Campaign groups such as Environmental Justice Foundation and Labour Behind the Label have recently lobbied on behalf of farmers in developing countries and garment workers in remote factories. Buying teams and sourcing /ethical trade teams in business need to be in much closer dialogue, as buyers are not always aware of the impact of the decisions.'
Black, 2008

Company members include Asda (Walmart-owned), Debenhams, Gap, Inditex (which owns Zara), Levi Strauss, Marks & Spencer, Monsoon, Mothercare, Next, New Look, Primark and Tesco.

Some fashion brands do far more than others in order to make the necessary changes and improve conditions for workers. Sourcing policy varies between different retailers and brands and although there are similar codes of practice to those of the ETI they are open to interpretation.

It is essential that retailers work closely with suppliers, giving them time and help in order to achieve the required standards. Monitoring suppliers, minimizing risk and solving short-term problems together can make fashion businesses more efficient as well as ethical. It may mean a rise in costs but should also mean an increase in sales and profit margins.

ETI base code

× Employment is freely chosen
× Freedom of association and the right to collective bargaining are respected
× Working conditions are safe and hygienic
× Child labour shall not be used
× Living wages are paid
× Working hours are not excessive
× No discrimination is practised
× Regular employment is provided
× No harsh or inhumane treatment is allowed

<www.ethicaltrade.org>

1   PRIMARK'S ETHICAL TRADE STRATEGY

In 2009, the ETI launched an inquiry on trade member Primark following allegations about workers' rights. Upon investigation, the ETI was satisfied that 'Primark is committed to a robust and credible ethical trade strategy. Where weaknesses remain, we are committed to working with the company to address them' (Dan Rees, director of the ETI).

1

Interview: Rob Hendry

ROB HENDRY

1984–present

sales director at Courtaulds. Courtaulds Textiles is Britain's largest producer of lingerie and underwear. The organization employs around 20,000 people across 16 countries in Europe, North America and Asia. It markets its products under leading retailer labels, such as Marks & Spencer and Walmart, as well as its own brands which include Aristoc, Berlei, Gossard and Well. Courtaulds is now owned by PD Enterprise Limited, a global garment company based in Hong Kong.

'Everyone moves the sourcing locations to where they believe it will be cheaper but you must also have available local raw materials to keep the costs down.'

Q How have you seen the supply chain change in the last decade?

A There is more direct sourcing between retailers and more factories that have the ability to work directly with retailers. Many fashion retailers have sourcing teams around the world set up to do this. Far less design and technical work is being carried out in the Europe and the USA and far more actioned in manufacturing (apart from specialist innovation where greater input is required).

Walmart is now working in partnership with Li & Fung rather than employing its own buyers and sourcing teams. I see that this type of joint relationship will increase in popularity and put the smaller operators out of business. However, a lot of SCM is also about cost reduction and what the retailer wants to pay, and they do not want to pay for expensive UK/EU/USA sales, sourcing offices and people in the supply chain. Many fashion retailers now believe they do not get many benefits from this.

Q How important are good relationships in supply chain outsourcing?

A I believe it is a priority; for example, Walmart and Li & Fung have now joined forces and it is often all about how good these partnerships are. Also, it is yet again down to cost savings and better value for money.

Q What do you consider are the main challenges?

A Cost and service are always paramount. Everyone keeps moving from country to country to try and get cost savings but we all know that the standard of living is increasing in the developing world and costs are going up all the time. China is now manufacturing more high-tech products than ever and the labour force is not what it was; they have suffered severe labour shortages in South China, which will lead to more manufacturing being moved out to the north of China for labour or to other countries nearby. I can see China being more dominant in the future.

Interview: Rob Hendry

Q What sort of pressure do you see on fashion retailers and suppliers?

A The main pressures and challenges are about cost, quality and delivery. Fabric costs have risen dramatically in the last six months. I am sure that all the manufacturers are asking for cost increases and in most cases the retailers pay more. It is important not to over-cost but just to add on the fabric increases to the selling price as retailers will always compare costs with other suppliers. This will also lead to some manufacturing programmes being switched from existing suppliers to new suppliers.

Q Do you think customers and retailers are willing to see any increase in prices?

A Yes, the costs will increase in the future, due to the raw material costs, and it is unavoidable that these will be passed on to the customers. The UK is seeing price movements in the high street now but the retailers will only take a hit on margins if they have no choice as most manufacturers do not have sufficient profit margin to take all of the extra costs. The amount of samples that retailers insist upon, which suppliers must send for testing and audits, all adds to the total cost of the goods. Freight costs have also gone up along with packaging costs. I am seeing that most developing countries are increasing the minimum wage structure.

'One key difference is that warehouse-style retail clubs are far bigger in the USA than in the UK and a lot of bargain sales are done via Sam's Club, Costco and BJ's – especially on designer brands.'

Q How do you think suppliers can improve service to retailers?

A Definitely by far the most important aspect is to improve the speed of response. Suppliers can control stock flow for retailers; they want us to be proactive and help them to merchandise, especially if we have local warehouse facilities. On the other hand, many retailers now want to buy apparel on a freight-on-board basis and control their own distribution centre or warehouse using logistics providers.

Critical path management is also a very good control as long as it is used correctly and everyone works within the set time controls.

Anyway, if you can see a saving that would help all parties in the supply chain then it should be promoted and used to everyone's advantage.

Q How easy or difficult do you think it is for fashion retailers to have complete visibility in the supply chain?

A They have more visibility now than ever; they either have their own sourcing hubs and quality assurance teams or they employ independent auditors. Retailers and buying teams spend a lot of time in factories now so the old days of taking contract and making it in a different location is much more difficult for manufacturers to get away with.

Interview: Rob Hendry

Do you see any differences in fashion supply chains between the USA and the UK?

Not a lot, to be honest. Import duty is critical but that applies to the UK or wherever in the world you are importing and exporting from and it is important to weigh up the options. Many of the same manufacturers will supply to USA and European fashion retailers and brands anyway.

'The majority of retailers have to be ethical – it's essential – but we all know some locations are more ethical than others.'

Q   **Which countries or locations do you see as the future for sourcing?**

A   This is the million dollar question. Everyone moves the sourcing locations to where they believe it will be cheaper but you must have available local raw materials to keep the costs down.

Vietnam, Cambodia, Pakistan, India and countries in Africa like Kenya and South Africa could grow the sourcing but that's a while away; the infrastructure is not there yet. China is still way out in front in terms of manufacturing and sourcing, in my opinion. Fabric and raw materials are a key issue at the moment and some mills will only quote a maximum of one month in advance.

As an example, the Pakistan government has just imposed a 15% duty on yarn exports and the fabric mills have stated they will move manufacture to Cambodia if they impose it! India has taken away the 7% export allowance. At the moment the locals want more clothes and if we are not careful we will have a shortage in fabrics due to demand, which in turn will create fewer exports and less business for all.

Q Do you think fashion retailers are concerned about being ethical?

A I think they have to be transparent on the outside and do all they can to ensure that they cannot be exposed. I am sure some of the suppliers are not transparent and ethical but the retailer can then transfer the blame if there are any issues: everyone has to sign agreements with big retailers. The majority of retailers have to be ethical – it's essential – but we all know some locations are more ethical than others to us in the West.

Q Will manufacturing ever return to being 'local', do you think?

A I do look at the UK but it's difficult: in a lot of cases they are using cheap and often illegal immigrants, which can be difficult to check. Manufacturing in the UK has almost disappeared unfortunately. If people are prepared to pay top prices then more UK and European manufacturing would be possible.

Fast response could also work, where say 70% is made at distance and 30% in local, and the retailer pays a different cost price. But again, you would need to ship all the fabric over from somewhere as there is little raw material production left in the UK.

'If customers only want to pay $1.00 for a T-shirt they should realize that it is not going to be made in an all-singing-and-dancing site.'

Case study: Walmart

Walmart was founded in 1962, with the opening of the first Walmart discount store in Rogers, Arkansas, USA. The company grew to 276 stores in 11 states by the end of the decade. In 1983, the company opened its first Sam's Club membership warehouse and in 1988 opened the first supercentre, now the company's dominant format. Walmart became an international company in 1991 when it opened its first Sam's Club near Mexico City. Today it is the largest global retailer and its sourcing and innovative processes have paved the way for many other retailers. One of its key statements for customers is 'every day low prices' (EDLP).

Sourcing strategy: Walmart with Li & Fung

Walmart formed a strategic alliance with Hong Kong sourcing expert Li & Fung within its global sourcing structure in a bid to reduce costs, improve quality and accelerate speed to market. Under the deal, Li & Fung formed a new company to manage the Walmart account and will act as a buying agent for goods valued at around $2 billion within the first year. Walmart's overall global sourcing strategy is to increase direct sourcing for the company's private brands.

Walmart also plans to set up global merchandising centres to align sourcing and merchandising and drive efficiencies across various merchandise categories including clothing. The retailer first announced a consolidated global sourcing structure centred on global merchandising centres at its annual investor meeting in 2009. By realigning its resources, leveraging its global scale and restructuring its relationship with suppliers, Walmart aims to drive significant savings across a supply chain that already spends $100 billion on private brand merchandise each year. This, in turn, will be seen in better quality at lower prices in its stores around the world. Walmart's new agreement with Li & Fung will bring benefits to both companies, each already a giant in its field. The agreement will help the retailer to cut costs and spread its global exposure and it could also double Li & Fung's business.

'Since our inception in 1983, our operating philosophy has remained the same – we work hard to be the buying agent for our members and deliver upon this agreement by eliminating unnecessary costs and maintaining a simple shopping environment.'
Sam's Club

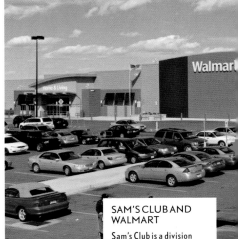

SAM'S CLUB AND WALMART

Sam's Club is a division of Walmart. Its mission statement is to eliminate unnecessary costs and maintain a simple shopping environment, passing on the savings to its 47 million members.

Sam's Club

A division of Walmart stores, Sam's Club is a warehouse club that sells branded goods at discount to customers who take up membership; it is an increasingly popular retail concept in the USA that is spreading globally. Sam's Club offers clothing brands through to homeware and products are developed via its many sourcing relationships and by maximizing its scale of global purchasing power.

Courtaulds Textiles

Courtaulds Textiles evolved around product innovation in the industrial revolution in the UK. It had factories for spinning, knitting and weaving within the UK and France, as well as finished goods manufacturing in the UK and it supplied and developed private label products to high-street retailers. In 2000, Courtaulds was acquired by Sara Lee Apparel, a US brand-led company, which bought the private label supplier for its product development expertise, to obtain access to its world-class Sri Lankan and Chinese manufacturing capabilities, and to increase market penetration in Europe. It has since been sold to PD Enterprise Ltd.

Courtaulds supplies branded apparel and lingerie to Walmart and Sam's Club. The company's product development team in the UK, in conjunction with US colleagues, was briefed to supply Sam's Club with a branded cashmere sweater line for a Christmas holiday promotion. This brief was built on Courtaulds' success in supplying the same product to George at Asda (a UK division of Walmart). Price targets for Walmart and Sam's Club are very low and volume is high.

Case study: Walmart

Sam's Club cashmere order

Price targets are set by the buyers and sourcing team from Sam's Club and samples requested by the buyers and global sourcing team. Walmart places a $2 million order for one sweater and the FOB dollar price from the factory is usually less than the average for a sweater in cashmere. The lead time for cashmere sweaters is around six months. Suppliers must meet Walmart's delivery schedules and inform the company about the production process via its WWRE (worldwide retail exchange) system.

Cashmere facts

× Cashmere goats in China and Inner Mongolia are the main source for raw cashmere fibres.
× The best fibre comes from the goats' underbellies.
× The longer and finer the yarn, the more expensive it is and the cashmere is carefully graded before spinning into yarn.
× Traditionally raw fibre was shipped to Scotland to be processed, spun, dyed and milled.
× The raw fibre of cashmere is fibre dyed, unlike most other yarns; this increases the lead times of the yarn and therefore the garments.
× The paler colours are the most expensive to produce as they require the paler and the purest raw material for dyeing.
× It takes the hair from three to four goats to make one sweater.
× Two-ply cashmere is the best quality because it pills less.
× Machine-washable cashmere, as seen on the high street, is blended and often given a silicone finish in order to make it suitable for machine washing. As with wool, this damages the fibre in the long term and it will felt, pill and shrink eventually. However, if it is cared for it will last for years.

CASHMERE SUPPLY CHAIN

China's manufacturing capacity has enabled a faster supply chain and cashmere is being produced in volumes never seen before. Retailers such as Walmart, M&S, Tesco, Gap and Uniqlo are driving down the cost to sell cashmere to the masses.

Cashmere supply chain

Thanks to China opening up the Inner Mongolia province, the source for the finest cashmere in the world, the sourcing process has been made much easier, which is why cashmere is now so widely available and, crucially, cheap. Cashmere has moved from a pure luxury item to an affordable fashion product, with a deluge of cheap and affordable cashmere on the high street. Traditionally cashmere had a slow supply chain, but as a result of international retailers seizing opportunities of global scale and purchasing power it is now available to the mass market.

In addition, large retailers have increased direct sourcing across the world, which means that the cost of using middlemen to source, ship and manufacture cashmere is reduced. Retailers are increasingly prepared to sell items such as cashmere on wafer-thin margins to attract shoppers.

In January 2005 the MFA agreement ended, which meant that quotas on textile imports from China were lifted, and China has invested heavily in its textile infrastructure. Cashmere fibres were never under quota, but China's massively enlarged manufacturing capacity means that cashmere is being produced in volumes never seen before. This has enabled Chinese manufacturers to ship the garments to eager retailers at a fraction of the historical price.

Walmart has set a trend for forward thinking in its supply chain activities. Now that it has joined forces with the sourcing giant Li & Fung it is likely that other innovative product developments will follow and influence the market as a whole.

'China has had a fundamental but subtle effect on the market. It is a ripple effect, because even if companies don't buy from China, everyone has to pull their socks up. Things that were unaffordable became affordable.'
Asda

Chapter 4 summary

This chapter has explored supply chain management (SCM) and its importance to the fashion business and merchandising. Successful companies are those that ensure their staff are well trained and aware of their impact on the supply chain, ensuring that the supply chain is working to its optimum capacity and efficiency. If fashion retailers and businesses get it right, SCM offers huge potential rewards.

Questions and discussion points

We have discussed the different issues associated with supply chain management. With this in mind, consider the following questions:

1. Consider a country or region you are most familiar with and analyse whether it is in a pre-industrial, industrial or post-industrial stage. What is the main form of employment: service industry or manufacturing?

2. Who are the biggest fashion retailers in your local shopping area? Do they display country of origin in the clothing sold? Visit several websites of fashion brands, review their CSR policy and compare with the ETI base code.

3. Do any fashion retailers you are familiar with have a code of conduct for suppliers displayed anywhere for customers to see? Investigate two very different brands and find out where they produce the goods. How transparent is the information provided?

4. Identify a number of fashion brands and find out where they are manufacturing; do they manufacture in China, Turkey or India, or all three?

5. Identify those designers who are using fair trade cotton or ethical fashion. How do they promote this? Identify who are the largest cotton producers and how much of it is fairly traded. Research cotton production in Uzbekistan.

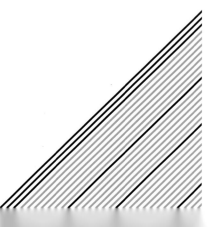

Exercises

We have seen how a continually changing world market presents major challenges for all fashion businesses. Retailers and clothing manufacturers must consider the impact of the supply chain as they continue to develop products and markets overseas. These exercises are designed to help you consider these issues in more detail:

1. Relationships in sourcing and logistics are vitally important. Discuss and review why this is true in global sourcing.

2. You are a buyer for a well-known denim brand. The fabric takes four weeks to produce in bulk and the garments take six weeks to produce, both in India. The shipping by sea to the USA adds another three to four weeks. Your CEO wants these new styles in stores in ten weeks. What can you do to change the lead time above? How can you achieve this? What impact will this have on the supply chain? What compromises may need to be made?

3. Consider the impact of the following risks upon supply chains:

   × A 5% increase in oil prices
   × A fabric supplier going out of business
   × An earthquake in the country making your goods
   × A lorry being hijacked and losing the contents
   × A designer leaving to join a competitor
   × Delivery of goods is one month late

   Which of these risks, in your opinion, is likely to have the greatest impact on your business and its supply chain? Score them for probability '1–10' and impact '1–10'.

1

BRANDING

5

This chapter explores some of the more exciting aspects of marketing and luxury branding. It examines some of the intangibles in the fashion business such as customer behaviour, brand identity and extension, brand equity and loyalty. In addition, it discusses advertising, the influence of the fashion press and the interaction between the media and designer brands. Finally, it examines a pressing concern for brands today: the scourge of counterfeit goods.

1 LUXURY BRAND:
   CHANEL

French fashion house Chanel
was founded by the couturier
Gabrielle 'Coco' Chanel in 1909.
It specializes in luxury goods
(haute couture, ready-to-wear,
handbags, perfumery and
cosmetics) with big budget
advertising campaigns driving
success through global expansion.

Customer profiling

Customer behaviour can be unpredictable and it is difficult to make assumptions about who will buy fashion, but it is probably safe to assume that customers can be promiscuous about purchasing habits and highly sophisticated in terms of taste. Consumers today are more affluent, discerning, demanding, cosmopolitan, educated and time-pressured than ever before.

Consumption

Consumption affects the general structure of demand and refers to the amount of specific goods consumed.

Customer behaviour is related to the customer's decision-making process, their wants and needs and their consumer type – see the box below. Analysing shopping behaviour examines the customer's response to the retail experience, choice of store and purchase decision.

Consumption also varies according to changes in society and differential growth in population. Changes in location of groups of customers within countries and sub-regions, in addition to cultural and regional tastes, can all affect consumption patterns within markets.

Consumer types

×   Need-driven customers; the activity is driven by need rather than preference. Consumers such as this are price-conscious.
×   Outer-directed customers form the bulk of the market. These consumers are concerned with status prosperity and getting ahead. They are concerned with products that 'say' something about them.
×   Inner-directed customers are few but growing in number. They are more flamboyant and individual; trendsetters from whom ideas diffuse to other groups.

'Positioning starts with a product. A piece of merchandise, a service, a company, an institution, or even a person... but positioning is not what you do to a product, it is what you do to the mind of the prospect... you position the product in the mind of the prospect.'
Ries & Trout, 1998

Lifestyle change

There have been ongoing changes in customer lifestyles, including population fluctuation. Population growth in northern Europe has slowed in the last 40 years. This is projected to decrease again. The lower birth rates are driven by reduced fertility rates and a change in social attitudes towards working women.

There has been a general rise in the volume of women in the workplace. In many countries, the growth rate has been maintained by migration patterns, especially in Europe (as a direct result of the changes in EU legislation). In the western world there are far more single households and people living alone; the total number of single households is rising.

This has many different implications, such as singles who have no children to look after and a higher disposable income but are sole breadwinners. The pre-retirement age group are active consumers with free time and money; this is evident in countries such as the UK and USA.

But what does all this mean? The broad-scale structure of customer consumption will continue to change over time. As income and occupations have changed, so too has expenditure on medical, entertainment, education and cultural activities. All of this creates opportunities and threats for retailers and the development of new service-related product markets. The key to success is to recognize and anticipate consumer change. Differences in customer attitudes and views are crucial to fashion retailers when devising product ranges and retail store formats. Lifestyle changes can create service opportunities but equally may create a shortage of employment in the future.

'Retail change has been driven in the past by the interaction of the consumer, retailer and government… [in] the future, the role of technology is increasingly important as an agent of change.'
Fernie, 1997

Positive effects of lifestyle change:

× More women in senior management
× Inheritance income
× Adoption of technology in the home has widened customer horizons and contributed towards the increase in travel
× Changed perceptions of shopping criteria and more options to purchase
× New product markets
× Transfer of consumer spending
× Higher expectations

Building a brand

Customer behaviour and marketing are at the very heart of fashion brands. There can often be a smoke and mirrors approach to advertising and marketing within the fashion business at times. Marketing fashion involves continual reinvention and rebranding to attract and entice customers.

Brand building begins with a clear definition of the target customer and the benefits of using a designer name. The advertising and promotion of a fashion brand should reflect an image that can promise customer satisfaction. Brand names are complex and they represent something special to each customer group – it is this combination of tangible and intangible factors that help create a certain image or association in the eye of the customer.

A designer name is usually a vital part of the selling, pricing, promotion and communication strategies; successful designers realize that they are involved in running a business that is a recognizable brand. According to Burt, Moore & Fernie (2000), 'Fashion design is synonymous with brand image. The marketing of fashion ensures that this shared international understanding of brand identity and meaning is developed and preserved through the standardization of communication strategies and strict control over merchandising, distribution and pricing.'

Smoke and mirrors

Smoke and mirrors may refer to any sort of presentation by which the audience is intended to be deceived, such as an attempt to fool a prospective customer into thinking that one has capabilities necessary to deliver a product in question.

'We don't want old tradition and stuffy design, but we want the richness of history. People are looking for the familiar and in heritage companies such as ours there is something reliable.'
Christopher Bailey, Burberry

2

1

1+2 BURBERRY AW11

The creative heads can help to shape and recreate a brand to ensure ongoing reputation and success. Burberry's creative director, Christopher Bailey, is largely responsible for reviving the company's brand image after it suffered a downturn.

Luxury brands

Most brands and fashion retailers aim to have an international or global presence, driven by home market saturation and the need to seek out new opportunities and customers. It is relatively straightforward to achieve, by showing on the runway and gaining coverage in the international press. In expansion terms this may make good strategy but it is fraught with difficulty in terms of understanding the market. Consumer taste outside of the home territory must be considered in order to succeed; being different is not always sufficient.

International retail can be a story of failure but, if there is sufficient investment and research into the local market, it can equal success. Luxury goods retailers are experts at this; in combination with big budget advertising campaigns the brand can drive success through global expansion.

Defining luxury brands

It is important to define what 'luxury' really means, particularly in fashion. A typical traditional luxury consumer is affluent and will appreciate quality and good value. For some consumers, luxury goods are very much a symbol of success; buying a luxury product is about displaying the ability to spend money and defining one's status.

Luxury means something different to everyone and it is important to define the market within which the brand operates and then examine what is meant by luxury within that market. An example of high-street luxury may be a blended cashmere sweater or a designer collaboration. Exclusivity of the product is also important and this can mean waiting lists for limited editions and customized products. When we are buying luxury goods we are sometimes buying a little bit of heritage; the DNA of the brand. The price is often irrelevant.

Success factors for inte

A successful brand ad
pressures and has th
collaborations and r
diffusion or bridge l
is also crucial to goc
This does not neces
should be cheap; ra
good value – every
development proc
to the brand. Focu   nds
and so is the legitin   y of the
brand. The luxury   . nas been
relatively slow to e   cial media and
online retailing bu   help consumers
to stay connected   e brand. Brand
extensions such as cosmetic and perfume ranges, eyewear or leather goods can build brands and help to spread the name. However, over-diversification and brand extension via licensing can cheapen and weaken a brand if not strictly controlled. This is why many luxury brands will not go down this route unless they spend time and effort investing in manufacturing and the supply chain.

1

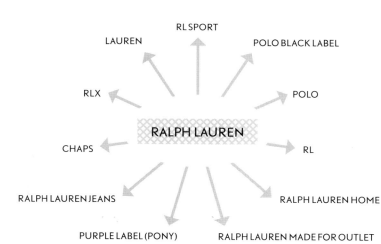

RL SPORT

LAUREN

POLO BLACK LABEL

RLX

POLO

RALPH LAUREN

CHAPS

RL

RALPH LAUREN JEANS

RALPH LAUREN HOME

PURPLE LABEL (PONY)

RALPH LAUREN MADE FOR OUTLET

2

1+2 RALPH LAUREN BRAND EXTENSION

Ralph Lauren is a good example of a company that uses the 'galaxy' model of brands. The company has a layered and differentiated brand offer, which includes homeware as well as fashion.

Luxury brands

Brand extension and layering

Brand extension and building is a lengthy process. It is essential to ask some key questions before a new range or product is developed, such as:

× Have we exhausted opportunities to grow in the existing market segment? If not, would this not be lower risk and quicker?
× Are we going to be distracted from the core business?
× Does our brand image 'fit' with the new products or new market?
× Will we still have economies of scale in the global market?
× Can we compete in the 'new' market with the existing competition?

Brands are continuously thinking of new and original ways to meet customers' needs. American fashion brands are expert at brand extension and have pioneered the creation of sub-brands. In the case of Ralph Lauren, the brand message is layered to create ranges of affordable luxury. These include diffusion and bridge lines, accessories and homewear ranges. However, brand layering is not an easy strategy and can lead to a proliferation of brands and labels from certain companies.

1

1 TOM FORD FOR GUCCI

Tom Ford was creative director at Gucci for ten years and turned around its fortunes in that time. When Ford left in 2004, Gucci Group was valued at $10 billion, having been almost bankrupt when he joined.

Brand value

The measurement of a brand and its value can determine the brand equity via image, reputation and loyalty. These are intangible qualities, which are difficult to measure, but can create great value for a brand. For example, a brand reputation can be built via the head or creative designer. Their reputation can make a difference to the brand image and therefore help to build brand equity. Tom Ford is a great example of this: he did much to build the reputation and brand name of Gucci. He is now an international brand name in his own right. Other well-known, influential, creative heads of design at large and international designer brands include: Christopher Bailey at Burberry; Karl Lagerfeld at Chanel; and Alber Elbaz at Lanvin.

These designers can help a brand assume value, both financially and in the eyes of the customer. The brand name can be one of the most valuable assets for a fashion business. The creative heads can ensure they keep the brand alive in the minds of the customers and equally help to shape and develop ongoing reputation and success.

Brand communication

Many retailers create marketing and retail environments to enhance their products. Beauty brands are very good at this, as are strong clothing and fashion ranges such as Abercrombie & Fitch and Victoria Secret. Consider brands that are easily identifiable thanks to their logos; those that promote an almost 'symbolic' value to customers.

Customers go through certain key stages when making or considering purchases. The AIDA model is often used in marketing to highlight the five key stages of a purchasing decision: awareness; interest; evaluation; trial; and adoption, which is the main aim of brands for customers to make a purchase from their offer. An effective brand communication strategy considers the effect on one or all of these stages.

Tom Ford at Gucci

Tom Ford was instrumental in turning around the Gucci brand:
× He transformed a dormant brand into a billion dollar empire
× Ford marketed and developed overtly sexual collections
× He created 'it' pieces, which were season-defining trends
× Ford presided over everything, including designing all aspects of the collection, marketing and advertising campaigns
× Ford established himself as an international taste-maker

Brand promotion

The fashion press creates the hype to shape and move brands via advertorial, editorials and big-budget advertising campaigns and features. The big designer brands and fashion houses spend millions of dollars on their advertising campaigns; in addition, they are increasingly using celebrities to promote their products. Such design houses have forged close relationships with the fashion press and media. The main international glossies, such as *Vogue* and *Harper's Bazaar*, create buzz and hype for certain designers and brands by covering the collections and featuring creative fashion editorial.

Fashion magazines are an essential promotional tool for fashion brands and building relationships with the important and influential fashion editors can be a crucial factor in brand success. Fashion editors and their teams attend and critique fashion collections and can make or break the designer label or brand if they write a poor review. Of course, the opposite is equally true! Designers need the exposure and the magazines need the advertising revenue, so it is a perfect match.

'Fashion is all about self-image and using brands as symbols that say something about how successful you are or want to be. Every successful brand is based upon image. The way you make the image is via advertising: fashion thrives on advertising; it creates the identity and the attraction.'
Fernie, Burt & Moore, 2000

1   **BRAND PROMOTION**

Big brands spend millions
of dollars on huge advertising
campaigns. Sisley and United
Colors of Benetton use
high-profile photographers for
their advertising campaigns,
which, in the case of Benetton,
are often provocative
and controversial.

1

Promotion in the fashion business

PR and promotion is an extremely important
tool in the industry; invaluable for building
good relationships between the brand and
the media. Recent developments in social
media such as Facebook and Twitter offer
inexpensive PR communication tools
for fashion brands; many companies take
advantage of it to increase the connection
with the customer and make them feel part
of the brand.

Celebrity culture

Many customers today are influenced by
celebrity culture and, in turn, celebrities'
wardrobes. The wealth of specialist
magazines available, such as *People* and
Hello, have a huge influence upon customer
spending and tastes. Good PR managers
understand the benefit of certain individuals
who are in the spotlight wearing designer
labels. Many fashion houses now use
celebrities in their advertising campaigns
to enhance brand equity, ensuring that
customers stay connected to the brand.

Brand protection

One of the downsides of mass-market production is the illegal copying of designer products and a developing black market industry of counterfeit goods. Customers want logos and certain brands in particular emblazon their products with a name or label, which has in effect contributed to the problem. It is difficult to prevent replication of products in an industry that thrives on trends and ideas and this problem has, to some extent, been driven by the international success and reputation of some brands.

It is also not just the luxury sector that suffers: in the mass market the lines between copying and selecting similar themes are extremely blurred. Fashion designers are often working on similar themes and have access to the same sources of inspiration and trends that are used as part of the range planning process.

The struggle between traditional high-street stores and cut-price rivals has reached a new level with the clothing chain Monsoon suing the discount retailer Primark over alleged copying. Primark was accused of selling replicas of six Monsoon designs. Monsoon claimed that the copies, which sold for a quarter of the price of the real thing, were of poor quality and as such, damaging to the Monsoon brand. Low-cost retailers are certainly capable of undercutting the mid-market stores by using cheap foreign labour and inferior materials – and by copying original designs.

One way that designers and brands can protect themselves is by trademarking their work and registering the logo and labels as their work. It should be a symbol of quality and authenticity. But high-street copies are much more difficult to protect – it is about design integrity and identity and is therefore much more intangible.

Taking steps

There are several organizations that designers can join in order to protect themselves and their products from replication. There are several luxury brand associations used to maintain integrity and to protect and promote luxury brands. In the UK there is an organization called The Walpole Group, which provides a community for the exchange of best practice ideas to drive business development in the UK and its export markets.

In France, a similar group is the prestigious Comite Colbert, of which many luxury brands such as Chanel, Dior, YSL, Hermès and Louis Vuitton are members. It acts in a similar fashion to Walpole in that it promotes its members and additionally encourages new French craftsmanship-led brands to flourish in a mass-produced world. It raises the global profiles of these renowned and iconic brands.

'When luxury brands went democratic they thought they could satisfy the middle market with lower priced bags. What they did not count on was mid-market consumers satisfying a craving for higher end items by buying fake versions they could pass off as real.'
Thomas, 2007

1   COUNTERFEIT
    HANDBAGS

The Counterfeit Museum
in Paris displays genuine
articles, such as luxury items,
pharmaceutical products,
computer software, spare car
parts and tobacco, alongside
their counterfeit copies to
demonstrate the differences
between the original and
the fake.

1

Interview: Nicky Lovell

NICKY LOVELL

1981–1993

menswear buyer at Selfridges

1994–1996

menswear buyer at Liberty of London

1996–1999

menswear buyer and concessions controller at Hoopers Ltd

1999–2007

product manager and retail development manager at McArthurGlen

2007–2010

head of client management at McArthurGlen, with a lead strategic role in developing and maintaining the company's relationships with its 750 brand partners across a portfolio of 18 designer outlet villages

2010–present

senior manager at Capital Shopping Centres

'The older customer is hugely significant in the rise of some brands and the re-emergence of Jaeger London and good, solid brands like Acquascutum, Crombie and Barbour.'

Q Which brands do you consider as currently influential in the market?

A There are still groups of cult brands such as Superdry that are everywhere, but I also see another wave of internationalization of many US brands that are targeting Europe and have expansion plans for the UK in particular. Some examples of these are Forever 21, Victoria Secret, Pottery Barn, Anthropologie, Coach, Therapy, Juicy Couture, Ellen Tracy and Kenneth Cole. The US brands are internationalizing further as the market has been hit by a lack of visitors due to currency fluctuation. Designer brands that have expanded into the Far East will be looking at the EU and the UK again.

Q Who are the new movers and shakers?

A Coach I think will follow in the footsteps of others like LV; customers are going to spend money on quality and value. The older customer is hugely significant in the rise of some of these brands and the re-emergence of Jaeger London and good, solid brands such as Acquascutum, Crombie and Barbour.

There is an emergence of Spanish brands: Springfield and Desigual are ones to watch, as well as luxury Spanish brands like Loewe and Cortefiel, the department store. They are looking for the right locations and new markets outside Spain. New formats and trial locations, such as pop-up shops, are a great idea to trial cities and products for all brands and spread the message wider.

Q How do you see luxury brands evolving?

A There is no doubt that there has been a trend for these to become more mainstream, which is fine so long as it does not devalue the brand. Tiffany has opened more stores in shopping malls, for example. The privately owned brands, such as Hermès and Chanel, are still true luxury brands. But many are looking for new markets and new customers.

Interview: Nicky Lovell

Q What differences do you see in customer behaviour?

A More considered purchasing; fast fashion may decline although Primark and Forever 21 do seem to go from strength to strength. The older affluent customer is important: relatively well-off customers will take longer to purchase but are loyal and want value for money. They need something that will last more than one season.

Q What regional differences have you noted in brand loyalty and consumer purchasing behaviour?

A Within the UK, for example, there are great regional differences; cities such as Glasgow, Newcastle, Liverpool and Leeds are quick to take up new brands and ranges. This is also true in other countries; certain locations will have customers hungry for the next new thing.

Q How do you see the future of high-street designer brands?

A Those designer collaborations are still going to develop. This creates brand exposure, spreads the name far and wide and creates hype for retailers. As a retail model it still has a way to go.

Q Does the strategy of luxury brands differ from the mainstream?

A Well, they have to go online and have been so slow to develop this, but it has to form a part of their retail format and offer to customers. Chanel is good at this; it produces a limited number of a new product – watches and bicycles, for instance – and once it is gone, it is gone. It is also important for the luxe brands to talk to each other and work together as a group: luxury goods conferences are on the increase.

'Location, private limited sales, trunk shows and internationalization are all important methods for designer brands to increase market share and build critical mass.'

Q Brand equity and loyalty: how do you think brands can change strategy and direction and continue to build and strengthen the brand and keep customers?

A Many brands are now working with artists and have sponsorships in place for exhibitions and so on, which can help bring brand equity. They also recognize that they need to go mass market but without dropping prices. It is a difficult balance.

Q What is your view on copying on the high street or counterfeit goods? What can be done about it?

A It is almost impossible to stamp out – at the end of the day it is a form of flattery! If the goods are more affordable they are not luxury, but if they are more affordable they will be less copied, so it is a double-edged sword.

Q How differently do you think designer brands operate in the USA to the UK/Europe?

A It is very different; currently there are different ranges per region, but this will change for all the right reasons of economies of scale and brand equity. Burberry, for example, is now producing a worldwide collection. This also helps to control the image across the globe and builds on internationalization strategy for the brands.

Interview: Nicky Lovell

Q Comite Colbert and Walpole: how useful are these to maintain brand integrity and craftsmanship?

A There is another: Altagamma in Italy does exactly the same job as these other two. They are very relevant and in Europe all of the key designer brands are a part of these groups. They form alliances so that when they want to internationalize they do it at the same time, controlled in the same locations. They build strength, and integrity and equity, creating little enclaves by being adjacent to each other in malls and city centres. Also, the three committees work closely together; they really do help each other out and cross-fertilize ideas and strategy.

Q Which new formats are the future for retailing, particularly fashion brands?

A Pop-up shops, as already mentioned, as well as online formats and outlets. Also now the online designer sales, such as Privé and Gilt Groupe. Net-a-porter now also has The Outnet and Mr Porter. Catalogues are still useful to some brands, to act as prompts to use websites, such as Boden and The White Company.

'New product development must continue to avoid becoming stale. The [brands] that take calculated risks may be the ones that win new customers.'

Q How crucial is location to designer brands?

A Location is really important but also private limited sales, trunk shows and internationalization are all important methods for designer brands to increase market share and build critical mass.

Q Do you think luxury brands should be online?

A Absolutely! But we must realize that different brands are at different stages with this – and they cannot ignore it.

Q What is the most important quality in terms of service that brands can bring?

A A common-sense approach and staff training is crucial; they must be able to understand fabrics and discuss with and advise customers. Retailers in the UK lack the US approach and expect staff to just pick it up; staff should be paid properly and rewarded with commission on sales.

Q How do you see the future for fashion brands?

A We need the markets to recover properly and also consolidation is needed for some brands. But new opportunities should still be considered; these are often the ones that build the future. New product development must continue to avoid becoming stale. The ones that take calculated risks may be the ones that win new customers.

Case study: Louis Vuitton

Louis Vuitton is part of the well-established LVMH group, run by Bernard Arnault. It is an international, travel-inspired company, with craftsmanship and attention to detail at its roots.

The paradox of Louis Vuitton is based upon fashion, travel, tradition, aspiration and exclusivity. Its consistent brand image and customer service sets it apart from other brands; dedicated to innovation and creativity, it blends art and commerce through collaborations.

Brand strategy

Louis Vuitton is a vertically integrated company, which means that it owns all of its manufacturing; this includes all the steps of the value chain. For example, it acquired an optical company in Switzerland to develop an eyewear range, rather than outsourcing to a manufacturer. The company has a long-term approach towards product development and investment as part of its brand strategy.

Louis Vuitton does not wholesale the brand; it controls all of its own stores, including those in department stores. Louis Vuitton controls profit and product and focuses upon delivering an exceptional customer experience. LVMH does not believe in brand synergy, so each brand owned by the company needs to stand alone and speak for itself creatively and financially.

'This product has value… it is worth every penny that you paid for it.'
Daniel Lalonde

Advertising

The company's advertising campaigns, as seen in *Vogue*, *Vanity Fair* and *Harper's Bazaar*, reflect its core values. They feature individuals in the campaigns such as Madonna, Mikhail Gorbachev, Keith Richards and Catherine Deneuve; people who have had 'rich personal journeys in life', which includes blending travel and the heritage of Louis Vuitton and its craftsmanship with fashion. Some of its other campaigns have replicated the movies, such as the famous scene on the railway track from the Alfred Hitchcock thriller *The Birds*.

Identifying the competition

Louis Vuitton believes that its main competition is luxury brands such as Hermès, Chanel and Dior (another LVMH brand). It also cites companies such as Apple, which may sound like a surprising comparison; however, Apple has similar brand values, an iconic product and name; and its customers have an equal emotional connection with the brand. They simply cannot live without the iPhone or Mac in the same way that a Louis Vuitton customer would not set foot on an aeroplane or out of the house without the bag or luggage.

Online presence

Like many other luxury brands, Louis Vuitton has been slow to embrace online retail. Transactional websites have been resisted in the luxury market partly due to the amount of copying and counterfeiting. However, establishing an online presence is a relevant way to build loyalty and increase customer satisfaction.

THE LOUIS VUITTON BRAND

Louis Vuitton, a trunk-maker in Paris since 1854, became renowned for creating luggage, bags and accessories. The company now produces ready-to-wear, shoes, watches, jewellery and sunglasses in addition to trunks and luggage.

Case study: Louis Vuitton

Counterfeits

Louis Vuitton is a widely copied brand. It has highly distinctive logos and trims on its products, the label is expensive and sought after as a status symbol and it is therefore open to counterfeiters. The company has a zero tolerance of copying and employs a worldwide team of lawyers in order to combat fraud. For example, it recently successfully fined the building owners who rented rooms to sellers of copied goods on Canal St in New York. The company also successfully pursued eBay when it was discovered that nine out of ten items sold on the site in 2007 were fake. The French courts ordered eBay to pay Louis Vuitton $63 million in compensation and it shut down 900 vendors on the site.

Marc Jacobs as creative director

Marc Jacobs is a graduate of Parsons School of Fashion in New York and he initially worked for Perry Ellis before launching his own label. Jacobs is a well-known 'bad boy' figure in the industry, so when Louis Vuitton hired Marc Jacobs in 1997, it was an undoubtedly risky move for Bernard Arnault. However, the risk paid off because Jacobs has been successful in revamping Louis Vuitton thanks to his collaborations with designers and artists such as Steven Sprouse, Takashi Murakami and Richard Prince. His work for Louis Vuitton has revived the label, appealing to a new, younger, customer base.

BRAND STRATEGY

Louis Vuitton successfully combines a strong brand development strategy with traditional craftsmanship. Continually expanding, the company has 17 production workshops, an international logistics centre and 450 shops around the world.

Retail formats

Louis Vuitton has 450 stores around the world, from Las Vegas to Mongolia. There are continual new plans for stores, each of which involves Marc Jacobs and his creative direction. Louis Vuitton maintains that it offers individual tailored and unique environments from New York to LA to Tokyo.

The most recent store is the new Bond Street flagship in London's West End. Designed by well-known architect and designer Peter Marino, the shop features extraordinary furnishings and unique visual merchandising to create a one-off store experience for customers.

Conclusion

Louis Vuitton is undoubtedly an iconic brand, which goes from strength to strength. It combines heritage, craftsmanship, luxury and a unique product with new and, at times, risky designs from its creative director. Its long-term approach to product development and brand extensions is carefully considered. Other fashion brands, luxury or otherwise, can learn from the Louis Vuitton success story.

Chapter 5 summary

Chapter 5 has examined some of the intangibles in the fashion business such as brand identity and extension, equity and loyalty. It looked at the influence of the fashion press, and its interaction with designers and brands, and how the advertising and promotion of a fashion brand should reflect an image for consumers to identify with. Finally, we examined the ways in which copying and counterfeiting affect fashion brands.

Questions and discussion points

We have discussed brand identity and extension, brand equity and the issues with counterfeit goods. With this in mind, consider the following questions:

1. How many brands can you think of that are widely copied and where have you seen copies or counterfeits sold?

2. Consider three designer brands and compare and contrast them. How many ranges or bridge lines do they have?

3. Think about brands that you consider to be new or up-and-coming in your region: why do you think they are so popular?

4. How do you think luxury brands can internationalize and stay in control of the brand and product?

5. Which brands do you not have access to that you would like to see in your local shopping area? Why? What is special about them?

Exercises

Brand value can be established via image, reputation and loyalty. These are intangible qualities that are difficult to measure but can create great value for a brand. The following exercises will help you to consider brand value in more detail:

1. Visit three different designer brands, preferably stand-alone stores. What differences do you see? Consider the following: product; price; visual merchandising.

2. Look at *Vogue* magazine and consider the advertising and press for different fashion brands; then compare this with another fashion magazine. What similarities and differences are there?

3. Customers and their shopping habits: visit your nearest shopping mall or high street in a large town or city. Observe the following:
   × Who is shopping there?
   × What age are they?
   × Are they fashionably dressed?
   × Speak to a few customers if possible and find out why they are shopping, for example, is it a special occasion; retail therapy; work and basics or for a replacement product?

4. Consider three luxury brands and compare and contrast the following:
   × History
   × Products
   × Price ranges
   × Store
   × Creative or head designer

   Put together a presentation showing the three that you selected and explain the points using a visual format.

CONCLUSION

This is a book about the fashion business. We have learned that the generic fashion cycle remains constant through the evolution of business trends and macro environments, while the ongoing analysis of the position and the environment of a fashion business is crucial to its future success. We have learned about the importance to stay ahead of key directions and emerging trends.

New roles and responsibilities in the fashion business are continually evolving. There are many training opportunities worldwide in colleges and universities for designers, buyers, merchandisers and technologists. To feed the growing industry it is important to consider the new type of roles and training needed in the future of fashion business; to nurture the talent coming through.

We have discussed how globalization is responsible for the development of the industry and that speed of innovation will not cease. It is likely that this will affect supply chains through the further consolidation of designers, retailers and manufacturers, forming close relationships to develop and innovate commercial garments. Globalization may also lead to further advances in mass customization and 'perfect fit' thanks to body scanning technology and digital imagery.

Collaboration via acquisitions and mergers in fashion retail is another growing business trend. Collaboration in fashion retailing is likely to result in the creation of more global super-brands and sourcers, such as Hong Kong agents Li & Fung.

At the other end of the scale, there is growing demand for individuality in the industry, leading to the rise of niche, original fashion brands. We only need look at the endurance of vintage fashion and the popularity of bespoke goods to see that not all customers seek out mass duplication and proliferation of similar fashion products. We must not lose sight of creativity in the fashion design and textile process: technology should aid the process and not replace skill, authenticity and true craftsmanship. Fashion has and always will have elements of originality and flair; it offers people the opportunity to stand out from the crowd. Whilst designers and fashion businesses are continually challenged to capture the zeitgeist, it is the constant turnover of new ideas that keeps fashion moving and these cannot be computer generated.

In the future, customers will continue to become even more demanding and search out the new and the different in product or service offerings. Alongside price, convenience is a crucial factor in the decision-making process. Whilst online and convenience shopping is important, the traditional bricks-and-mortar stores will never disappear. Shopping still remains a leisure activity and fashion retailers and brands should not lose sight of that. Fashion is a commodity and fulfils a need but those brands and fashion retailers prepared to go further – those with superior service and innovative products – will be the winners. A solid business model will ensure success, with those who take calculated risks gaining competitive advantage. Essentially, fashion will always be driven by the desire for the 'must-have' as well as fulfilling a need.

Glossary

AIDA model

Attention, interest, desire and action.
A customer awareness model developed
by E St Elmo Lewis in the 1890s.

Baby boomers

Those born after the Second World War
when birth rates rose dramatically.
Baby boomers are generational cohorts.

Bespoke

Made to measure.

Bridge lines

Designer ranges that occupy a mid-market
level; they are cheaper than ready-to-wear.

CAD

Computer-aided design.

CFDA

Council for Designers of America.

Comparative shopping

Shopping as analysis of the competition.

Concessions

Shop within a shop such as a brand in
a department store.

Cool hunters

Marketing professionals who observe
and predict forthcoming and existing
cultural trends.

CPFR

Collaborative planning forecasting and
replenishment; a system used by retailers.

CRM

Cause-related marketing. A collaboration
between a business and a not-for-profit
organization, such as a charity.

CSR

Corporate social responsibility.
The self-regulation of a business within legal,
ethical and international standards.

DC

Distribution centre or warehouse.

Design brief

Used by a design team or compiled
by designers in conjunction with
merchandising and buying departments.

Diffusion line

A cheaper designer range, it may be
ready-to-wear or high-street fashion.

Directional shopping

Shopping trips taken to gain ideas and
inspiration.

Direct supply

The supply of goods direct from factory
to retailer.

E-commerce

The online sale of goods.

EDI

Electronic Data Interchange: the electronic transmission of data between organizations.

EPOS

Electronic point of sale.

ETI

Ethical trade initiative: an alliance of companies, trade unions and voluntary organizations.

Fast fashion

High-street interpretation of designer trends produced using a short supply chain model.

FOB

Freight on board: this specifies whether the buyer or seller pays for the shipment and loading costs and at which point responsibility for the goods is transferred.

FSV

Full service vendor: a company that takes an active design role and all responsibility for manufacturing and logistics.

Generational cohort

A term used in demographic profiling, a generational cohort is a group of individuals who share the experience of common historical events.

Generation X

The generation born after the post-World War II baby boom, from the 1960s through to the early 1980s.

Good, better, best

A pricing matrix used by retailers when planning ranges.

Haute couture

Bespoke high fashion.

Key pieces

Must-have items within a seasonal range.

Megatrends

Macro environmental trends.

MFA

Multi Fibre Arrangement: established in 1974 to govern world trade in textiles and garments. It expired on 1 January 2005.

Micro trend

Fashion trend that is usually not much more than a fad; lasts weeks not months.

Middlemen

Agents for manufacturers, acting as go-betweens.

Glossary

Mood boards

Initial design ideas in a visual format, used in the design and range planning process.

Multi-channel retailer

Company that sells its goods through various formats, such as online and bricks-and-mortar stores.

NGO

Non-governmental organization: a not-for-profit organization that operates independently from any government.

OPP

Opening price point: a retail promotion strategy used to lure customers in.

OTB

Open to buy: a flexible budget strategy that enables merchandise to be ordered later on in a buying season.

Outlet

Discount malls selling designer end-of-lines or made-for-outlet products.

Own brands

Retailers' brands designed in-house. Also known as private label.

PESTEL

Political, economic, sociological, technological, environmental and legal analysis: a framework for the macro environment.

Pop-up shop

Short-term outlet used by brands to trial a location.

PR

Public relations: the practice of promoting public image of an organization or an individual using topics of interest and news items that provide a third-party endorsement and do not direct payment.

Prêt-à-porter

Ready-to-wear designer fashion.

Product development

The development of initial ideas into actual garments.

Product mix

Based upon the marketing mix and part of range planning.

QR

Quick response: a manufacturing model developed by the Japanese, the basis of a fast-fashion supply chain.

Range planning

Process used to plan a commercial collection.

Retail therapy

Shopping for leisure.

RTW

Ready to wear.

Runway

The showcase of designer collections. Also known as a catwalk.

Sampling

Process of making initial prototype samples; forms part of range planning.

SBO

Sales-based ordering: the use of EPOS data to generate an order for future stock requirements.

Smart fabric

Fabric with a special finish, such as waterproof or technical fabrics for sportswear.

Social media

Online interaction through websites such as Twitter or Facebook.

Specification (spec) sheet

Technical garment diagram supplied to manufacturers.

SWOT

Strengths, weaknesses, opportunities and threats: an internal business analysis model.

The seven Ps

The marketing mix.

USP

Unique selling point: a feature of a company or product that differentiates it from similar companies or products.

Vintage

Retro or antique fashion with value.

WTO

World Trade Organization: an organization that intends to supervise and liberalize international trade.

WWRE

Worldwide retail exchange: an alliance that enables members to source products electronically.

Zeitgeist

Spirit of the moment.

Bibliography

Bell, D
The Coming of Post-Industrial Society
Basic Books, 1987

Bevan, J
The Rise & Fall of Marks & Spencer… And
How it Rose Again
Profile Books, 2007

Black, S
Eco-Chic: The Fashion Paradox
Black Dog Publishing, 2006

Borden, N H
The Concept of the Marketing Mix
1965

Brannon, E L
Fashion Forecasting: Research, Analysis,
and Presentation
Fairchild Books, 2005

Christopher, M
Logistics and Supply Chain Management
Financial Times/Prentice Hall, 2007

Easey, M
Fashion Marketing
John Wiley and Sons, 2002

Gladwell, M
The Tipping Point: How Little Things Can
Make a Big Difference
Abacus, 2008

Goworek, H
Fashion Buying
John Wiley and Sons, 2007

Hale, A and Wills, J
Threads of Labour
Wiley-Blackwell, 2002

Hamel, G and Prahalad, CK
Competing for the Future
Harvard Business School Press, 1994

Jackson, T and Shaw, D
Mastering Fashion Buying & Merchandising
Management
Palgrave Macmillan, 2005

McGoldrick, P
Retail Marketing
McGraw-Hill Higher Education, 2002

Porter, M
Competitive Advantage
Free Press, 1996

Ries, A and Trout, J
Differentiate or Die: Survival in Our Era of
Killer Competition
John Wiley and Sons, 1992

Thomas, D
Deluxe: How Luxury Lost its Lustre
Penguin, 2007

Trott, P
Innovation Management and New Product
Development
Financial Times/Prentice Hall, 2007

Tungate, M
Fashion Brands: Branding Style from Armani
to Zara
Kogan Page, 2006

Vejlgaard, H
Anatomy of a Trend
McGraw-Hill, 2007

Useful websites

www.acid.eu.com

www.arcadiagroup.co.uk

www.belindarobertson.com

www.burberry.com

www.businessoffashion.com

www.coolhunting.com

www.datamonitor.com

www.drapersrecord.com

www.ethicaltrade.org

www.fakesareneverinfashion.com

www.guardian.co.uk

www.harrods.com

www.jcpenney.com

www.labourbehindthelabel.org

www.louisvuitton.com

www.marksandspencer.com

www.mcarthurglen.com

www.mintel.com

www.nytimes.com

www.peclersparis.com

www.promostyl.com

www.prospects.ac.uk

www.ralphlauren.com

www.samsclub.com

www.sjk.com

www.style.com

www.thecoolhunter.net

www.trendhunter.com

www.vogue.com

www.walmart.com

www.wgsn.com

www.wwd.com

Index

Index

Compiled by Indexing
Specialists (UK) Ltd

Acknowledgements and picture credits

With special thanks

I would like to thank all friends and colleagues who have helped me with this book and, in particular, those involved in the fashion business who have given up their time for interviews: Belinda Dickson OBE, George Sharp, Nicky Lovell, Rob Hendry and Kim Mannino.

Thanks also to Toni Bergmeier, Gordon Message, Jane Yates, Jane Grove and, in particular Elaine Swift, for her invaluable help with proofreading and editing.

Last but not least, AVA Publishing: managing director Caroline Walmsley and Rachel Parkinson for their support throughout this process. And thank you to my parents, who encouraged me to pursue a career in the fashion business all those years ago and supported my education.

credits

p 12 Rex Features
p 13 © Victoria and Albert Museum, London
p 14 Catwalking.com
p 24 courtesy of Peclers Paris
p 27 courtesy of Peclers Paris
p 76 Tupungato / Shutterstock.com
p 78 Ragne Kabanova / Shutterstock.com
pp 94–95 Catwalking.com
p 111 Ragne Kabanova / Shutterstock.com
p 120 Michael Dunlea / Rex Features
p 138 Catwalking.com
p 143 Catwalking.com
p 145 Sipa Press / Rex Features
p 146 Catwalking.com
p 151 Sipa Press / Rex Features
p 158 (top) Stephanie Paschal / Rex Features; (bottom) Sipa Press / Rex Features
p 159 Richard Young / Rex Features
p 160 (top) Sipa Press / Rex Features; (bottom) Paul Cooper / Rex Features
p 161 (top right) Tupungato / Shutterstock.com

BASICS
FASHION MANAGEMENT

Lynne Elvins
Naomi Goulder

Working with ethics

Publisher's note

The subject of ethics is not new, yet its consideration within the applied visual arts is perhaps not as prevalent as it might be. Our aim here is to help a new generation of students, educators and practitioners find a methodology for structuring their thoughts and reflections in this vital area.

AVA Publishing hopes that these **Working with ethics** pages provide a platform for consideration and a flexible method for incorporating ethical concerns in the work of educators, students and professionals. Our approach consists of four parts:

The **introduction** is intended to be an accessible snapshot of the ethical landscape, both in terms of historical development and current dominant themes.

The **framework** positions ethical consideration into four areas and poses questions about the practical implications that might occur. Marking your response to each of these questions on the scale shown will allow your reactions to be further explored by comparison.

The **case study** sets out a real project and then poses some ethical questions for further consideration. This is a focus point for a debate rather than a critical analysis so there are no predetermined right or wrong answers.

A selection of **further reading** for you to consider areas of particular interest in more detail.

Ethical: awareness/ reflection/ debate

Working with ethics

Ethics is a complex subject that interlaces the idea of responsibilities to society with a wide range of considerations relevant to the character and happiness of the individual. It concerns virtues of compassion, loyalty and strength, but also of confidence, imagination, humour and optimism. As introduced in ancient Greek philosophy, the fundamental ethical question is: *what should I do?* How we might pursue a 'good' life not only raises moral concerns about the effects of our actions on others, but also personal concerns about our own integrity.

In modern times the most important and controversial questions in ethics have been the moral ones. With growing populations and improvements in mobility and communications, it is not surprising that considerations about how to structure our lives together on the planet should come to the forefront. For visual artists and communicators, it should be no surprise that these considerations will enter into the creative process.

Some ethical considerations are already enshrined in government laws and regulations or in professional codes of conduct. For example, plagiarism and breaches of confidentiality can be punishable offences. Legislation in various nations makes it unlawful to exclude people with disabilities from accessing information or spaces. The trade of ivory as a material has been banned in many countries. In these cases, a clear line has been drawn under what is unacceptable.

But most ethical matters remain open to debate, among experts and lay-people alike, and in the end we have to make our own choices on the basis of our own guiding principles or values. Is it more ethical to work for a charity than for a commercial company? Is it unethical to create something that others find ugly or offensive?

Specific questions such as these may lead to other questions that are more abstract. For example, is it only effects on humans (and what they care about) that are important, or might effects on the natural world require attention too?

Is promoting ethical consequences justified even when it requires ethical sacrifices along the way? Must there be a single unifying theory of ethics (such as the Utilitarian thesis that the right course of action is always the one that leads to the greatest happiness of the greatest number), or might there always be many different ethical values that pull a person in various directions?

As we enter into ethical debate and engage with these dilemmas on a personal and professional level, we may change our views or change our view of others. The real test though is whether, as we reflect on these matters, we change the way we act as well as the way we think. Socrates, the 'father' of philosophy, proposed that people will naturally do 'good' if they know what is right. But this point might only lead us to yet another question: *how do we know what is right?*

You
What are your ethical beliefs?

Central to everything you do will be your attitude to people and issues around you. For some people, their ethics are an active part of the decisions they make every day as a consumer, a voter or a working professional. Others may think about ethics very little and yet this does not automatically make them unethical. Personal beliefs, lifestyle, politics, nationality, religion, gender, class or education can all influence your ethical viewpoint.

Using the scale, where would you place yourself? What do you take into account to make your decision? Compare results with your friends or colleagues.

Your client
What are your terms?

Working relationships are central to whether ethics can be embedded into a project, and your conduct on a day-to-day basis is a demonstration of your professional ethics. The decision with the biggest impact is whom you choose to work with in the first place. Cigarette companies or arms traders are often-cited examples when talking about where a line might be drawn, but rarely are real situations so extreme. At what point might you turn down a project on ethical grounds and how much does the reality of having to earn a living affect your ability to choose?

Using the scale, where would you place a project? How does this compare to your personal ethical level?

01 02 03 04 05 06 07 08 09 10

01 02 03 04 05 06 07 08 09 10

Your specifications
What are the impacts of your materials?

In relatively recent times, we are learning that many natural materials are in short supply. At the same time, we are increasingly aware that some man-made materials can have harmful, long-term effects on people or the planet. How much do you know about the materials that you use? Do you know where they come from, how far they travel and under what conditions they are obtained? When your creation is no longer needed, will it be easy and safe to recycle? Will it disappear without a trace? Are these considerations your responsibility or are they out of your hands?

Using the scale, mark how ethical your material choices are.

Your creation
What is the purpose of your work?

Between you, your colleagues and an agreed brief, what will your creation achieve? What purpose will it have in society and will it make a positive contribution? Should your work result in more than commercial success or industry awards? Might your creation help save lives, educate, protect or inspire? Form and function are two established aspects of judging a creation, but there is little consensus on the obligations of visual artists and communicators toward society, or the role they might have in solving social or environmental problems. If you want recognition for being the creator, how responsible are you for what you create and where might that responsibility end?

Using the scale, mark how ethical the purpose of your work is.

01 02 03 04 05 06 07 08 09 10

01 02 03 04 05 06 07 08 09 10

One aspect of fashion management that raises an ethical dilemma is how to tackle the issue of cheap replica goods. Counterfeit products flood markets on the back of successfully marketed brands. Fraudsters can copy and reproduce new products so quickly that fakes are often available before the original. Brand designers can add specialist detailing to help identify a genuine product, but consumers do not necessarily notice it. Research shows that over 70 per cent of British consumers would knowingly purchase counterfeit clothing or footwear if the price and quality were acceptable. People often see counterfeiting as a victimless crime in which the seller is purely saving consumers from over-priced products sold by rich companies. How much responsibility should a fashion manager take when imitations are produced by unscrupulous manufacturers and demand is driven by consumers? Even if fashion managers wish to eliminate the trade of counterfeit brands, what might they most usefully do?

In 1955, Mary Quant opened Bazaar on King's Road, London. Situated in the Royal Borough of Kensington and Chelsea, the local clientele were wealthy young professionals, artists and actors. It was one of the first boutiques of its kind, stocked with new and interesting clothes targeted at the youth market. Its success drove Quant to create her own audacious designs that played with conventions, including the miniskirt.

Skirts had been getting shorter since the late 1950s – a development Quant considered to be practical and liberating. Although short skirts were also created by other designers, it was Quant who coined the term 'miniskirt' and it became an emblem of rebellion for the post-war generation who rejected the beliefs of their parents. With hemlines as high as eight inches above the knee, the miniskirt was, for many, a celebration of women's pride and assertion. But for others, it gave the impression that the wearers were sexually available and served to objectify women for voyeuristic men.

Alongside her designs, Quant created a recognisable brand identity featuring a daisy logo and countless images of her distinctive hairstyle. By 1966, she was working with numerous manufacturers and the commercial appeal of her lines enabled Quant to secure deals with American chain stores. In Britain, Quant set up her own label, which was available across 160 department stores.

The miniskirt of the swinging '60s stayed in vogue until the end of the decade. The Society for the Preservation of the Miniskirt demonstrated outside Christian Dior's fashion show because the collection featured a return to long coats and dresses but as the Vietnam War escalated, and the future looked less positive, the miniskirt fell out of fashion. Hemlines came back down to the ankle in a maxi style.

In 1966, the president of Tunisia announced that miniskirts were to be legally banned and other nations followed suit. In some countries, the wearing of hot pants has been held to constitute a judicial incitement to rape and in 2000 miniskirts were outlawed in Swaziland because it was believed that wearing them encouraged the spread of AIDS. More recently, in 2010, the mayor of an Italian beach town ordered police officers to fine women wearing miniskirts as part of their battle to 'restore urban decorum and facilitate better civil co-existence'.

Is it unethical to create clothing that makes women look sexually appealing?

Would you allow your young daughter to wear a miniskirt?

Is commercial success in fashion based on design or the ability to create a brand and negotiate business deals?

I believe in that one-on-one sell. I don't really believe in flooding the market with loads of goods that don't mean much.

Alexander McQueen

AIGA
Design Business and Ethics
2007, AIGA

Eaton, Marcia Muelder
Aesthetics and the Good Life
1989, Associated University Press

Ellison, David
Ethics and Aesthetics in European Modernist Literature:
From the Sublime to the Uncanny
2001, Cambridge University Press

Fenner, David E W (Ed)
Ethics and the Arts:
An Anthology
1995, Garland Reference Library of Social Science

Gini, Al and Marcoux, Alexei M
Case Studies in Business Ethics
2005, Prentice Hall

McDonough, William and Braungart, Michael
Cradle to Cradle:
Remaking the Way We Make Things
2002, North Point Press

Papanek, Victor
Design for the Real World:
Making to Measure
1972, Thames & Hudson

United Nations Global Compact
The Ten Principles
www.unglobalcompact.org/AboutTheGC/TheTenPrinciples/index.html